W9-CUO-972

QUICK PRACTICE
WRITING SKILLS
Grades 6-8

> Dozens of Reproducible Pages
> That Give Kids Practice
> in Grammar, Mechanics, Spelling,
> and Other Key Writing Skills

by Marcia Miller and Martin Lee

NEW YORK • TORONTO • LONDON • AUKLAND • SYDNEY
MEXICO CITY • NEW DELHI • HONG KONG • BUENOS AIRES

SCHOLASTIC
Teaching
Resources

Cover design by Maria Lilja
Cover illustration by Mike Gordon
Interior design by Jeffrey Dorman
Interior illustrations by Marcy Ramsey

ISBN 0-439-37097-3
Copyright © 2003 by Marcia Miller and Martin Lee
All rights reserved.
Printed in the U.S.A.

1 2 3 4 5 6 7 8 9 10   40   09

CONTENTS

ABOUT THIS BOOK

As teachers, we want to guide students to become good writers, to empower them to communicate in writing as freely, naturally, and effectively as they do when speaking.

> **Quick Practice Writing Skills: Grades 6–8** is one of a series of four grade-specific books for students K–8. Each book has a dual purpose—to sharpen students' skills as writers, and to provide ways you can help to prepare them for success when they take standardized tests of writing.

Because writing is such a crucial measure of one's ability to communicate, many school districts and state departments of education utilize approved lists of writing standards at each grade level that students are expected to meet. Writing has increasingly become a regular component of standardized testing. In addition to short-answer items, standardized tests ask students to plan, write, edit, and present a finished piece of independent writing on a given topic.

> **Quick Practice Writing Skills: Grades 6–8** gives students opportunities to practice and develop some of the key skills and strategies of the writing process. By using this book, your students will grow as writers.

Good writing doesn't happen by chance. We become skilled writers because we write—and keep on writing. We write to express fact, opinion, humor, memory, feelings, admiration, criticism, and creativity. We write to instruct, inform, and interpret. The more we write, the more we understand about writing. We learn to mold a piece of writing to a given purpose, to fit a particular audience, and to achieve a certain result.

> **Quick Practice Writing Skills: Grades 6–8** addresses the many ways that standardized tests may evaluate students' ability to express themselves as writers.

The activity pages you will find in *Quick Practice Writing Skills: Grades 6–8* are based on recent versions of an assortment of testing instruments, as well as a compilation of standards applied to language arts and writing. They provide various formats and levels of complexity within the targeted grade range. Each page or activity is self-contained and concise enough to be used as a warm-up or follow-up to a related lesson within your writing curriculum. While some activity pages have questions with only one correct answer, others are open-ended, mirroring many of the newer standardized tests.

In developing these books, we have drawn upon a wide range of materials and resources. One very useful Web site you may wish to explore can be found at **www.mcrel.org**. Here, you can examine a wealth of materials about standards-based education in general as well as specific curriculum standards, testing, and position papers.

> **Quick Practice Writing Skills: Grades 6–8** can help your students develop greater confidence and feel more relaxed in a test-taking situation.

Test taking is like any task—the more it is practiced, the less daunting it becomes. The activities in this book cannot substitute for the standardized testing instruments your students will take, as mandated by your school district and/or state education department. But they can decrease some of the anxiety and mystery surrounding standards and standardized testing.

USING THIS BOOK

Quick Practice Writing Skills: Grades 6–8 has been organized into four main sections that reflect the general aspects of writing:

> **1.** Grammar and Mechanics
>
> **2.** Writing Styles
>
> **3.** The Writing Process
>
> **4.** Writing Activities

Within each section, we address a particular aspect of writing in quantifiable and grade-appropriate ways. Obviously, in a book of this length, it is not possible to test everything, nor can one book be certain to dovetail with every aspect of your particular writing curriculum or the standards your students are expected to meet. Simply regard the sections as broad-stroke plans of organization.

Standardized writing tests include short-answer and free-form writing tasks. In this book we include both. You will find certain writing skills exercised in short-answer items. You will also find ample opportunities for open-ended writing, especially in section 4.

At the back of the book, you will find a Writer's Self-Evaluation Checklist, which students can use as an aid to refine their writing. You will also find selected answers and brief teacher notes.

Here are some suggestions for using Quick Practice Writing Skills: Grades 6–8

- Present the activity pages in any order you wish.

- Allow pages to be completed independently, in pairs, in small groups, or by the whole class as a group activity. Use your best judgment.

- You may wish to read directions aloud to remove a potential stumbling block for less-independent readers.

- You might wish to do a sample exercise together, as you see fit.

- Feel free to take any format we provide in this book and revise it to fit your students' needs. Use any exercise as a springboard for similar activities you create, or extend and develop it into a complete lesson or project.

- Take the time to review and discuss students' responses. Analyze the responses for diagnostic use.

- Print and distribute (or post) the Tried & True Test-Taking Tips on page 6. Take time to talk about them with your class. Invite students to add their own useful suggestions to the list.

TRIED & TRUE TEST-TAKING TIPS

- Get plenty of rest the night before the test.
- Eat a healthy breakfast.
- Wear comfortable clothing.
- Get to school on time!
- Gather all the materials you need—sharp pencils, erasers, scratch paper, and so on.
- Bring your positive attitude!
- Listen to or read instructions carefully.
- If you don't understand something, raise your hand and ask for help.
- Work purposefully and carefully.
- Read the whole question and all the given answer choices before marking anything.
- Don't let other people distract you. Stick to the task.
- Try to answer ALL questions. But if you are stumped, take a deep breath and move on. Come back to the question later.
- If you change your mind, erase your first answer completely.
- If you aren't sure, choose the answer that seems best to you.
- Double-check your answers, if you have time.
- Proofread your writing.
- Neatness counts! Make sure that all your writing is legible.

PART 1:

GRAMMAR
AND MECHANICS

SENTENCES AND SENTENCE PROBLEMS

Choose the best description for each group of words.

1. Last week's meeting of world leaders.
- Ⓐ simple sentence
- Ⓑ compound sentence
- Ⓒ complex sentence
- Ⓓ run-on sentence

2. The meetings took place in the new convention center.
- Ⓐ simple sentence
- Ⓑ compound sentence
- Ⓒ complex sentence
- Ⓓ sentence fragment

3. Until everyone arrived, the diplomats chatted in groups of two's and three's.
- Ⓐ simple sentence
- Ⓑ compound sentence
- Ⓒ complex sentence
- Ⓓ run-on sentence

4. The leaders took their seats and listened to the speaker at the podium.
- Ⓐ simple sentence
- Ⓑ compound sentence
- Ⓒ complex sentence
- Ⓓ sentence fragment

5. The leaders met for two hours, they then ate a sumptuous dinner.
- Ⓐ run-on sentence
- Ⓑ compound sentence
- Ⓒ complex sentence
- Ⓓ sentence fragment

6. When the dinner was over, some diplomats attended a play.
- Ⓐ simple sentence
- Ⓑ compound sentence
- Ⓒ complex sentence
- Ⓓ run-on sentence

7. Near where the hotels were located and not too far from the convention center.
- Ⓐ run-on sentence
- Ⓑ compound sentence
- Ⓒ complex sentence
- Ⓓ sentence fragment

8. The host country made every effort to treat the visitors graciously.
- Ⓐ simple sentence
- Ⓑ compound sentence
- Ⓒ complex sentence
- Ⓓ run-on sentence

9. The meetings lasted for three days; they were seen by many as a great success!
- Ⓐ simple sentence
- Ⓑ compound sentence
- Ⓒ complex sentence
- Ⓓ run-on sentence

10. The participants agreed to meet again, they set up a committee to choose the time and place.
- Ⓐ run-on sentence
- Ⓑ compound sentence
- Ⓒ complex sentence
- Ⓓ sentence fragment

Name ....

WRITE COMPLETE SENTENCES

Use each fragment to write a complete sentence. You may position the fragment anywhere in your sentence.

1. looking out the window

_____

2. that she had to drive

_____

3. when we left the exhibit

_____

4. running as fast as he could

_____

5. traveling all night by bus

_____

6. as long as we're here

_____

7. under a jumble of papers

_____

8. without fully understanding the directions

_____

9. immediately stopped writing and looked up

_____

10. in the waning afternoon light

_____

WRITE SENSIBLE SENTENCES

Read each set of sentences. Then choose the sentence that best combines them.

1. **Roosevelt Junior High has a new soccer coach. His name is Mr. Franklin.**

   (A) Roosevelt Junior High has Mr. Franklin, a new soccer coach.

   (B) His name is Mr. Franklin and he is the new soccer coach at Roosevelt Junior High.

   (C) Mr. Franklin is the new soccer coach at Roosevelt Junior High.

   (D) Roosevelt Junior High has a soccer coach: Mr. Franklin is his new name.

2. **Hannah is on the gymnastics team. Hannah practices floor exercises before school each morning.**

   (A) Hannah practices floor exercises before school each morning and she is on the gymnastics team.

   (B) Hannah, who is on the gymnastics team, practices floor exercises before school each morning.

   (C) Before school each morning, Hannah practices floor exercises and is on the gymnastics team.

   (D) On the gymnastics team, Hannah practices floor exercises before school each morning.

3. **There are thirteen players on the school basketball team. Six of the players are sophomores.**

   (A) Six of the players on the school basketball team are sophomores and there are thirteen players on the team.

   (B) There are thirteen players on the school basketball team and six sophomores.

   (C) There are thirteen players on the school basketball team but only six sophomores.

   (D) Of the thirteen players on the school basketball team, six are sophomores.

4. **The Douglass High baseball team is simply awful. Attendance at home games is very low.**

   (A) Attendance at Douglass High home games is very low and the baseball team is simply awful.

   (B) Because the Douglass High baseball team is simply awful, home attendance is very low.

   (C) Simply awful Douglass High has very low baseball attendance at home games.

   (D) The Douglass High baseball team is simply awful because attendance at home games is low.

5. **Allen is a quarterback. Allen goes to Linton High. Allen is a senior.**

   (A) Allen is a quarterback and he plays for Linton High and he is a senior.

   (B) Allen goes to Linton High and he is a quarterback and a senior.

   (C) Allen, a senior, is a quarterback for Linton High.

   (D) Allen is a quarterback who is a senior and plays for Linton High.

Name ....

FIX RUN-ON SENTENCES

Fix each run-on sentence using one or more of these methods:

- **Use an end mark to separate it into two sentences.**
- **Use a comma and an appropriate conjunction to join the two clauses.**
- **Use a semicolon to form a compound sentence.**

1. The Olympic symbol is five rings, each a different color, linked to represent five geographic regions, the symbol also stands for the friendship of the competing nations.

2. The first Summer Olympic Games were held in 1896, the first Winter Olympic Games were in 1924.

3. The Olympics has a motto, the motto is *Citius, Altius, Fortius*, it means "swifter, higher, stronger" in Latin.

4. Jesse Owens won four medals in track and field in the 1936 Olympics in Berlin, even more dramatic, Bob Beamon broke the long-jump record by nearly two feet in the Olympics in Mexico City in 1968.

5. In the 1896 Games, the winning time in the 100-meter dash was 12 seconds, in 2000, the winning time was 9.87 seconds.

6. The luge became a Winter Olympic event for the first time in 1964, Thomas Keohler of East Germany won the men's event, Ortun Enderlein of Germany was the women's winner.

7. Snowboarding became an Olympic event in 1998 there were four categories: men's giant slalom, men's halfpipe, women's giant slalom, and women's halfpipe.

8. The 1980 Summer Olympic Games were boycotted by sixty-two countries, including the United States, the 1984 Games were boycotted by the Soviet Union and most Eastern bloc nations.

9. Michael Johnson of the United States won gold in the 200-meter run in the 2000 Olympics, in the 1996 Games he won gold in that event and in the 400-meter run, too.

10. In 1908 and 1920, figure-skating events were held in the Summer Olympics in 1908 and 1920 ice hockey was also part of the Summer Olympics.

11. In Sydney, Australia, in 2000, Marion Jones of the United States won five medals it was the most ever won by a woman track athlete.

12. As of 2002, the Winter Olympic Games have been held twice in Austria, Switzerland, Japan, and Norway, three times in France, they have been held four times in the United States.

Name ....

COMMON NOUNS AND PROPER NOUNS

Write a proper noun that is an example of each common noun.

Write a common noun that is an example of the class to which each proper noun belongs.

1. city _____

2. writer _____

3. lake _____

4. composer _____

5. government official _____

6. building _____

7. baseball player _____

8. bridge _____

9. actor _____

10. board game _____

11. state capital _____

12. national park _____

13. mountain _____

14. automobile _____

15. movie _____

16. song _____

17. Hungary _____

18. Georgia O'Keeffe _____

19. Langston Hughes _____

20. Orion _____

21. Detroit Tigers _____

22. South America _____

23. Kobe Bryant _____

24. Toyota _____

25. Mariah Carey _____

26. New Mexico _____

27. Nile _____

28. February _____

29. *The Great Gatsby* _____

30. *Hamlet* _____

31. Yankee Stadium _____

32. Thomas Edison _____

Name ....

IDENTIFY KINDS OF NOUNS

Read each group of words. Decide whether the underlined word or words is a common noun, a proper noun, a collective noun, or not a noun at all. Write the correct letter.

> A. common noun   C. collective noun
> B. proper noun   D. not a noun

_____ **1.** at <u>El Tovar Hotel</u>

_____ **2.** on the <u>trail</u> to the Colorado River

_____ **3.** the <u>crowd</u> gathering at the Visitor Center

_____ **4.** during the ranger's <u>nightly</u> talk

_____ **5.** in a picnic <u>area</u> near Wupatki National Monument

_____ **6.** at a <u>stopping place</u> half-way down Bright Angel Trail

_____ **7.** near the <u>lookout</u> by the water station

_____ **8.** addressed the attentive <u>audience</u>

_____ **9.** explored by Civil War <u>veteran</u> John Wesley Powell

_____ **10.** along <u>Grandview Trail</u>

_____ **11.** by the <u>river</u> near Phantom Ranch

_____ **12.** the <u>committee</u> formed to study the new dam

_____ **13.** gliding along in a <u>rubber</u> raft

_____ **14.** stayed in a <u>cabin</u> on the North Rim

_____ **15.** land belonging to the <u>Hopi</u>

_____ **16.** along the border between <u>Arizona</u> and Utah

_____ **17.** assisted by a <u>team</u> of rangers

_____ **18.** according to the diary <u>Powell</u> kept

_____ **19.** walked out to the <u>rim</u>

_____ **20.** wait by the side of the trail for the mules to <u>pass</u>

❋ CONNECT

Write one sentence that contains a common noun, a proper noun, and a collective noun. Identify each type of noun.

_____

_____

NOUNS: GENERAL, SPECIFIC, AND MORE SPECIFIC

Nouns can be more or less specific. When you write, use specific nouns wherever possible to help make your ideas more precise. Complete the chart. The first row has been done as an example.

	GENERAL NOUN	SPECIFIC NOUN	MORE SPECIFIC NOUN
1.	vehicle	car	sport utility vehicle
2.	animal	bird	
3.	clothing	pants	
4.		uncle	Uncle Ralph
5.		bread	rye
6.	technology		
7.	entertainment		
8.		soda	
9.		novel	
10.	movie		
11.			*60 Minutes*
12.			Donald Duck

✳ C O N N E C T

Choose something you have recently written. Find the general nouns in your piece. Does each one present the picture you intended? If not, replace that noun with a more specific one.

USE ABSTRACT NOUNS

Abstract nouns refer to ideas rather than to things you can see, hear, smell, taste, or touch. Write the letter of the abstract noun that best completes each sentence.

1. She overcame her _____ and spoke out loudly and clearly before the large group.
    a. happiness   **b.** shyness   **c.** greed   **d.** arrogance

2. Following years of bloody conflict, all wished for _____ between the warring factions.
    a. hopelessness   **b.** greed   **c.** peace   **d.** danger

3. As a result of a thorough watering, the parched plant came to _____.
    a. life   **b.** evil   **c.** intelligence   **d.** wealth

4. When the beloved ruler died, _____ reigned in the land.
    a. generosity   **b.** hopefulness   **c.** happiness   **d.** sadness

5. Respected by all for her _____, the senator has been reelected time after time.
    a. carelessness   **b.** honesty   **c.** greed   **d.** poverty

6. The miner had been trapped for eight days; _____ for his survival dwindled hourly.
    a. fear   **b.** satisfaction   **c.** hope   **d.** glamour

7. The ethics of the renowned historian, not his _____, was at issue after he was accused of plagiarism.
    a. intelligence   **b.** beauty   **c.** misery   **d.** wealth

8. The captain's _____ was admired by all who fought with him.
    a. silliness   **b.** health   **c.** callousness   **d.** bravery

9. After a surprise victory in the Olympic Games, _____ was instantly hers.
    a. grief   **b.** fame   **c.** mirth   **d.** curiosity

10. The majestic _____ of Yosemite National Park has awed visitors for generations.
    a. hostility   **b.** love   **c.** beauty   **d.** depth

Name _____

USE PRONOUNS

Write the letter of the pronoun that best completes each sentence.

1. The company of Civil War reenactors pitched _____ tents by the creek.
   a. his   **b.** their   **c.** them   **d.** they

2. Each of the men woke early and began to fix _____ simple breakfast.
   a. their   **b.** we   **c.** his   **d.** her

3. As the lieutenant of the company, it fell to _____ to address the men regarding the day's events.
   a. us   **b.** them   **c.** I   **d.** me

4. I informed them of _____ first assignment: to practice marching. Everyone groaned.
   a. they   **b.** our   **c.** your   **d.** his

5. Reenactors don't like marches, but _____ exercises are a daily part of soldiers' lives.
   a. these   **b.** them   **c.** that   **d.** this

6. After marching, I told them, "Listen up, men, _____ is what we will do next."
   a. that   **b.** these   **c.** this   **d.** it

7. The firing demonstration, _____ is the activity the men enjoy the most, was next.
   a. who   **b.** which   **c.** whom   **d.** that

8. One reenactor, _____ was obviously uncomfortable, lagged behind the rest.
   a. whom   **b.** whose   **c.** who   **d.** which

9. He is a "soldier" _____ I respect, so I wondered what his problem was.
   a. whom   **b.** who   **c.** which   **d.** what

10. "My wool uniform really itches," he admitted. "And _____ can appreciate that!"
   a. none   **b.** anyone   **c.** nobody   **d.** both

PRONOUNS AND ANTECEDENTS

Choose the antecedent that matches the underlined pronoun.

1. Fifth Avenue in New York City is more than a street; <u>it</u> is the most expensive shopping street in the world.

    a. street   **b.** New York City

    b. Fifth Avenue   **d.** world

2. Stores on Fifth Avenue pay the highest retail rents in the world. <u>These</u> can be more than $550 per square foot.

    a. stores   **c.** rents

    b. world   **d.** Fifth Avenue

3. New York City is also home to Macy's, <u>which</u>, at 2.15 million square feet, is the world's largest department store.

    a. Macy's   **c.** home

    b. New York City   **d.** department store

4. The United States has more shopping malls than any other country. If <u>they</u> are counted along with all of America's drug, discount, or supermarket centers, the total number of shopping centers exceeds 40,000.

    a. stores   **c.** United States

    b. countries   **d.** shopping malls

5. The world's largest toy-store chain is Toys 'Я' Us. Although these stores are based in New Jersey, the biggest single <u>one</u> is located in England.

    a. toy-store chain   **c.** toy store

    b. New Jersey   **d.** toy

6. Do you like going to a garage sale? <u>It</u> is an experience many regularly enjoy.

    a. a garage   **c.** an experience

    b. going to a garage sale   **d.** you

7. Although <u>it</u> lasted only two days, the White Elephant Sale at the Cleveland Convention Center raised more than $400,000.

    a. $400,000

    b. elephant

    c. White Elephant Sale

    d. Cleveland Convention Center

8. The world's largest underground shopping center is in Toronto, Canada. <u>It</u> has more than 16 miles of shopping arcades.

    a. Toronto   **c.** miles

    b. Canada   **d.** shopping center

Name ....

USE PRONOUNS CORRECTLY

Read each sentence. Check the pronoun usage. If there is no error, circle *Correct*. If there is an error, circle *Incorrect*.

1. Her seat is in the orchestra, but mine seat is
in the mezzanine.

      Correct   **Incorrect**

2. Whom has the tickets for tonight's
performance?

      Correct   **Incorrect**

3. Alexander and me are sitting in the
same row.

      Correct   **Incorrect**

4. Some of the audience members left their
seats during the play.

      Correct   **Incorrect**

5. Each person in the play thought they were the star performer.

      Correct   **Incorrect**

6. Miranda sat between Jacques and me during the first act.

      Correct   **Incorrect**

7. Miranda told Jacques and myself all we would need to know to understand
the play.

      Correct   **Incorrect**

8. However, I think he and I could have gotten along just fine without her help.

      Correct   **Incorrect**

9. Us students are going to put on a show of our own: We'll write the songs
and routines, do our own choreography, and make the costumes.

      Correct   **Incorrect**

10. Except for you and her, all of our friends will take part in the show.

      Correct   **Incorrect**

✸ CONNECT

Reread those sentences that are *incorrect* as written.
Then fix each one without changing its meaning.

Name ....

IDENTIFY THE SIMPLE PREDICATE

Mark the letter beneath the word that is the simple predicate.

1. Karen <u>wants</u> to record an <u>album</u> of six <u>songs</u>.
    Ⓐ   Ⓑ   Ⓒ   Ⓓ

2. <u>She</u> <u>chooses</u> a studio <u>with</u> bargain <u>rates</u>.
    Ⓐ   Ⓑ   Ⓒ   Ⓓ

3. She <u>booked</u> three <u>hours</u> of studio <u>time</u>
        Ⓐ   Ⓑ   Ⓒ

weeks in <u>advance</u>.
        Ⓓ

4. <u>At</u> last, the <u>exciting</u> <u>day</u> <u>arrived</u>.
    Ⓐ   Ⓑ   Ⓒ   Ⓓ

5. Once <u>in</u> the studio, Karen <u>lost</u> time <u>getting</u> acquainted with the <u>equipment</u>.
        Ⓐ   Ⓑ   Ⓒ   Ⓓ

6. By the <u>end</u> of the three hours, <u>she</u> <u>barely</u> <u>completed</u> one song.
       Ⓐ   Ⓑ Ⓒ   Ⓓ

7. <u>But</u> that one <u>song</u> <u>impressed</u> the studio's <u>engineer</u> and producer.
    Ⓐ   Ⓑ   Ⓒ   Ⓓ

8. Karen <u>wondered</u> <u>how</u> to <u>finance</u> the rest of her <u>project</u>.
        Ⓐ   Ⓑ   Ⓒ   Ⓓ

9. She <u>offered</u> to <u>work</u> for the producer in <u>exchange</u> for more studio <u>time</u>.
      Ⓐ   Ⓑ   Ⓒ   Ⓓ

10. <u>He</u> <u>happily</u> <u>agreed</u> to her <u>idea</u>.
    Ⓐ Ⓑ   Ⓒ   Ⓓ

11. <u>In</u> the end, <u>Karen</u> <u>spent</u> fourteen hours <u>making</u> her music.
    Ⓐ   Ⓑ   Ⓒ   Ⓓ

12. And she <u>improved</u> her telephone and <u>bookkeeping</u> <u>skills</u> in the <u>process</u>.
        Ⓐ   Ⓑ   Ⓒ   Ⓓ

USE THE RIGHT VERB FORM

Write the letter of the correct verb form to complete each sentence.

1. If you are like most people, you _____ certain "rules of thumb" in your everyday life.

    a. applying   **c.** apply

    b. applied   **d.** to apply

2. For instance, you know that it makes sense _____ for a few extra minutes of travel time on days when the weather is bad.

    a. allowing   **c.** allow

    b. to allow   **d.** to have allowed

3. Have you ever _____ how to tell if a letter weighs more or less than an ounce?

    a. wondering   **c.** wonder

    b. to wonder   **d.** wondered

4. One quick way to know is to compare the weight of your letter with the weight of five quarters, which _____ about an ounce.

    a. weighing   **c.** are weighing

    b. have weighed   **d.** weigh

5. A rule of thumb for predicting how someone is likely to behave in the future is to examine how they _____ in the past.

    a. behaving   **c.** have behaved

    b. behave   **d.** will behave

6. If you are an experienced traveler, you probably know that it _____ your body about one day to adjust for each time zone you cross in your travels.

    a. took   **c.** was taking

    b. takes   **d.** has taken

7. As a rule, do you find that you _____ more money food shopping if you shop when you are hungry?

    a. spent   **c.** spended

    b. spending   **d.** spend

USE LINKING VERBS

The most common linking verb is *be*. Choose the correct form of *be* to complete each of the related sentences that follow.

1. Last summer, my sister and I _____ visiting our friend, who lives in the country.
    a. are
    b. was
    c. were
    d. have been

2. One day—it _____ a Tuesday—we walked up the hill to the crumbling old barn.
    a. has been
    b. would be
    c. may have been
    d. was being

3. We spotted there a blue truck that _____ parked in a dirt lane behind the barn.
    a. is
    b. was
    c. were
    d. are

4. Our friend, who goes past the barn frequently, said that the truck _____ there for weeks.
    a. were
    b. is being
    c. is
    d. had been

5. An elderly man was sitting in the truck. "He _____ sitting there each time I passed by," my friend said, "and he never moved."
    a. be
    b. has been
    c. had been
    d. was

6. "What _____ behind this guy's unusual behavior?" I wondered.
    a. shall be
    b. should be
    c. might be
    d. will have been

7. "Oh, we _____ too suspicious," my friend replied. "The old fellow probably has a perfectly good reason for parking by the barn and just sitting there."
    a. be
    b. was being
    c. had been
    d. are being

FORMS OF ADJECTIVES AND ADVERBS

Complete the chart to show how the modifiers change form to compare *two* people, places, or things, or to compare *more than two* people, places, or things. The first row has been done as an example.

Degrees of Modifiers

	POSITIVE	COMPARATIVE	SUPERLATIVE
1.	soft	softer	softest
2.	high	higher	
3.	speedy		speediest
4.	little	less	
5.		more painful	most painful
6.	sharp		sharpest
7.	slowly	more slowly	
8.		more cautious	most cautious
9.	good		
10.		worse	worst
11.	friendly		
12.	flexible		
13.		more shallow	
14.	easy		
15.			most powerful

✱ C O N N E C T

Choose a modifier that does not appear in the chart. Then write a sentence that correctly uses two forms of that same adjective or adverb.

USE PREPOSITIONAL PHRASES

When you write, use prepositional phrases to add details and to make relationships clear. Notice how the underlined prepositional phrase makes the following sentence more descriptive:

Pitchers and catchers begin their spring training early, before the other players arrive.

Rewrite each sentence to make it more descriptive. Add one or more prepositional phrases.

1. The veteran players greeted one another warmly.

_____

2. The rookies walked onto the practice field.

_____

3. Several delighted fans watched the players practice.

_____

4. A coach watched his star pitcher take warm-up tosses.

_____

5. The manager hoped that his first baseman was again healthy.

_____

6. The outfielders caught flies, made throws, and ran.

_____

7. The players stretched and did calisthenics.

_____

8. The owner and general manager watched everything closely.

_____

9. One player was talking to a reporter.

_____

10. Leaning, another player waited for his turn on the massage table.

_____

Name ....

Read each sentence. Choose the underlined word that is spelled incorrectly.
If there are no spelling errors, choose "No Error."

1. America <u>certainly</u> has <u>it's</u> share of wonderful and <u>weird</u> <u>museums</u>. *No Error*
           (A)   (B)   (C) (D)   (E)

2. A <u>group</u> of <u>mischievous</u> <u>seenyers</u> found Connecticut's Nut Museum <u>amusing</u>. *No Error*
    (A)   (B)   (C)   (D)   (E)

3. In my <u>vue</u>, the <u>oddest</u> <u>exhibits</u> are in the <u>Cockroach</u> Hall of Fame in Texas. *No Error*
        (A)   (B)   (C)   (D)   (E)

4. <u>Newscasters</u> <u>often</u> <u>prefer</u> the <u>permanant</u> collection at the Mutter Museum. *No Error*
    (A)   (B) (C)   (D)   (E)

5. The <u>committee</u> <u>scheduled</u> a visit on the <u>eighth</u> to the <u>Desert</u> Museum of Maine. *No Error*
      (A)   (B)   (C)   (D)   (E)

6. A <u>dilemma</u> for Museum of Bad Art
    (A)

    <u>personnel</u> is <u>whether</u> or not to give
    (B)   (C)

    <u>oppinions</u>.   *No Error*
    (D)   (E)

7. <u>Generally</u>, one <u>should</u> <u>attempt</u> to go
    (A)   (B)   (C)

    to the Cookie Jar Museum on a

    full <u>stomach</u>.   *No Error*
    (D)   (E)

8. Do <u>villains</u> and <u>theives</u> find
    (A)   (B)

    <u>excursions</u> to the Old Jail Museum <u>instructive</u>?   *No Error*
    (C)   (D)   (E)

9. Are <u>haircuts</u> <u>advised</u> for <u>almost</u> all those <u>privaledged</u> to visit the Barber Museum? *No Error*
     (A)   (B)   (C)   (D)   (E)

10. I <u>doubt</u> that <u>adolescents</u> <u>wood</u> <u>appreciate</u> the Merry-Go-Round Museum. *No Error*
      (A)   (B)   (C)   (D)   (E)

11. The Liberace Museum <u>celabrates</u> the <u>entertainer's</u> <u>extravagant</u> <u>possessions</u>. *No Error*
                  (A)   (B)   (C)   (D)   (E)

12. The <u>First</u> Century Museum <u>appeals</u> to <u>individuals</u> interested in <u>ancient</u> history. *No Error*
      (A)   (B)   (C)   (D)   (E)

FIND CAPITALIZATION ERRORS

Read each sentence. Choose the underlined word that is either capitalized incorrectly or is not capitalized but should be. If all words are capitalized correctly, choose "No Error."

1. <u>Thomas</u> Jefferson and John <u>Adams</u>
Ⓐ   Ⓑ
were <u>Political</u> <u>rivals</u> and longtime
     Ⓒ   Ⓓ
friends. *No Error*
        Ⓔ

2. Adams was the <u>second</u> <u>U.S.</u>
            Ⓐ   Ⓑ
president and <u>Jefferson</u> was the
          Ⓒ
<u>Third</u>. *No Error*
Ⓓ   Ⓔ

3. Adams, from <u>Braintree</u>, <u>Massachusetts</u>,
          Ⓐ   Ⓑ
<u>graduated</u> from <u>Harvard</u> in 1755.
Ⓒ   Ⓓ
No Error
Ⓔ

4. Jefferson, the son of a wealthy
<u>planter</u>, read <u>Greek</u> and <u>latin</u> and
Ⓐ   Ⓑ   Ⓒ
played the <u>violin</u>. *No Error*
      Ⓓ   Ⓔ

5. Adams joined the <u>Federalist</u> <u>party</u>,
             Ⓐ   Ⓑ
while <u>Jefferson</u> was a
    Ⓒ
<u>Democratic-Republican</u>. *No Error*
Ⓓ   Ⓔ

6. Jefferson succeeded Patrick <u>Henry</u>
                     Ⓐ
as <u>governor</u> of <u>Virginia</u>. <u>he</u> resigned in
    Ⓑ   Ⓒ   Ⓓ
1781. *No Error*
        Ⓔ

7. Adams was the <u>Country's</u> <u>first</u> <u>vice</u>
            Ⓐ   Ⓑ   Ⓒ
<u>president</u>, a post he believed to be
Ⓓ
trivial. *No Error*
      Ⓔ

8. In 1800, Jefferson and <u>Aaron</u> <u>Burr</u>
                 Ⓐ   Ⓑ
got the same number of <u>Electoral</u>
                  Ⓒ
<u>college</u> votes. *No Error*
Ⓓ   Ⓔ

9. <u>Adams</u> lived for a <u>quarter</u> <u>century</u>
Ⓐ   Ⓑ   Ⓒ
after he left <u>office</u>. *No Error*
        Ⓓ   Ⓔ

10. <u>Jefferson</u> established the <u>University</u>
Ⓐ   Ⓑ
of <u>Virginia</u> in his beloved <u>State</u>. *No Error*
   Ⓒ   Ⓓ   Ⓔ

11. <u>Adams</u> and <u>Jefferson</u> died on the
Ⓐ   Ⓑ
same <u>day</u>—<u>July</u> 4, 1826! *No Error*
     Ⓒ   Ⓓ   Ⓔ

12. They died on the <u>fiftieth</u>
               Ⓐ
<u>Anniversary</u> of the <u>Declaration</u> of
Ⓑ   Ⓒ
<u>Independence</u>. *No Error*
Ⓓ   Ⓔ

CORRECT PUNCTUATION ERRORS

Each sentence below lacks *one or more* punctuation marks. Correctly insert the appropriate end marks, commas, colons, semicolons, quotation marks, dashes, or apostrophes.

1. Donald who generally eats only burgers and pizza won a prize of a dinner for himself and three friends at a gourmet restaurant.

2. Which of my pals should I invite Donald wondered.

3. After some thought he settled on Juan Julie and Pat.

4. The only one of the four with a more sophisticated palate than Donald was Pat whose diet also included pasta, tacos, and even some vegetables.

5. For dinner at the city's top-rated restaurant each friend dressed up and looked fantastic

6. Wow Juan exclaimed when he saw the limo pull up to take them to their meal.

7. Julies first problem at the restaurant was not knowing which fork to use for the first course stuffed mushrooms and baby sweet pickles.

8. Actually no one in the group was ever sure which utensil to use with each of the five courses.

9. Finally the dessert arrived a chocolate mountain floating in a lake of raspberry sauce.

10. On the next day while the four friends waited in line at a fast-food joint, they agreed that last night's main course couldve used some ketchup.

Name ....

COMPLETE THE SENTENCE: HOMOPHONES

Complete the sentence by circling the correct word in each pair.

1. The Cats are in the tournament! **(Their, They're)** playing in the West Regional.

2. They now have the chance to continue their **(rain, reign)** as national champions.

3. The team flies to Albuquerque, the **(sight, site)** of the first-round games.

4. Albuquerque is the **(capital, capitol)** of New Mexico.

5. The players are excited and **(all ready, already)** for their first opponent.

6. So are the coach and his **(assistance, assistants)**, who have been preparing for this all season.

7. The Cats had hoped to **(crews, cruise)** through their first game.

8. But through the **(coarse, course)** of that hard-fought contest, the score went back and forth.

9. When the other team **(missed, mist)** a desperate last-second shot, the Cats won.

10. All the players and their fans **(side, sighed)** with relief.

11. But the fact that the game against a weak opponent was so close was not a good **(sign, sine)**.

12. The coach preached **(patience, patients)** and predicted a tough road ahead for his team.

13. He reviewed each player's **(role, roll)** in the upcoming game against a much tougher opponent.

14. "**(Your, You're)** going to have to play smarter to win this one," he told his rattled players.

15. "Let's **(review, revue)** what we know about our next opponent and what we need to do to beat them," he continued.

16. As they listened to the coach, the players' confidence began to **(soar, sore)**.

17. "**(Weave, We've)** come too far to lose now!" one player shouted.

18. That attitude struck a **(chord, cord)** with the other players.

19. Although they started sluggishly, the confident Cats soon turned a close game into a **(rout, route)**!

20. "No celebrating yet, boys," the coach cautioned. "We **(meat, meet)** an even tougher team in our next game."

WRITE A SENTENCE: HOMOPHONES

Use each pair of homophones in a single sentence.

1. for, four

_____

2. blue, blew

_____

3. cent, sent

_____

4. its, it's

_____

5. close, clothes

_____

6. principal, principle

_____

7. ad, add

_____

8. have, halve

_____

9. boarder, border

_____

10. hour, our

_____

11. desert, dessert

_____

12. council, counsel

_____

WHAT'S WRONG WITH THE SENTENCE?

Each sentence below contains one kind of error—or no error at all. Choose the best answer.

1. So, do you think you know all the state capitals.

- (A) capitalization error
- (B) spelling error
- (C) punctuation error
- (D) no error

2. Is Omaha or Lincoln the Capital of Nebraska?

- (A) capitalization error
- (B) spelling error
- (C) punctuation error
- (D) no error

3. Which is the capital of South Carolina: Columbus or Columbia?

- (A) capitalization error
- (B) spelling error
- (C) punctuation error
- (D) no error

4. Phoenix, the capital of Arizona, is in the dessert, isn't it?

- (A) capitalization error
- (B) spelling error
- (C) punctuation error
- (D) no error

5. Is Californias capital its biggest city?

- (A) capitalization error
- (B) spelling error
- (C) punctuation error
- (D) no error

6. If your in Oklahoma's capital, what city are you in?

- (A) capitalization error
- (B) spelling error
- (C) punctuation error
- (D) no error

7. Is Boise the correct way to spell the capital of Idaho?

- (A) capitalization error
- (B) spelling error
- (C) punctuation error
- (D) no error

8. There's a Springfield in nearly every state, but only won is a state capital.

- (A) capitalization error
- (B) spelling error
- (C) punctuation error
- (D) no error

PART 2:

WRITING STYLES

IDENTIFY THE TONE

Writers look at their topics in many different ways. For each sentence, choose the tone that best describes the writer's view.

1. The doctor's behavior was out of line and his attitude was totally unprofessional, to say the least.

    Ⓐ encouraging   Ⓑ angry   Ⓒ casual   Ⓓ sarcastic

2. I had the best time baby-sitting for the twins last night—both kids were sick and crying and they were up forever, too.

    Ⓐ serious   Ⓑ instructive   Ⓒ sarcastic   Ⓓ scornful

3. The ambassador sits at your right; be sure to sit only once she is seated and to address her as "Madam Ambassador."

    Ⓐ awesome   Ⓑ scholarly   Ⓒ humorous   Ⓓ formal

4. "I owe everything to my math teacher," the award-winning student said, beaming. "He gave me the confidence I'd lacked."

    Ⓐ appreciative   Ⓑ serious   Ⓒ sarcastic   Ⓓ casual

5. "So, dude, you didn't tell me in your e-mail—where are all our fans meeting us later?"

    Ⓐ instructive   Ⓑ humorous   Ⓒ casual   Ⓓ sarcastic

6. According to an article in a recent edition of the respected journal *Archaeology*, there is evidence that the rapid changes that signaled the transformation of the Honshu culture also had a measurable effect on neighboring groups.

    Ⓐ serious   Ⓑ encouraging Ⓒ respectful   Ⓓ scholarly

7. When you write a paragraph, you should make an effort to vary your sentence types, lengths, and structures.

    Ⓐ ironic   Ⓑ serious   Ⓒ instructive   Ⓓ casual

8. When they saw the photo of me grinning and holding the trophy, my parents nearly exploded in delight, while my little sister was totally envious.

    Ⓐ sarcastic   Ⓑ joyful   Ⓒ humble   Ⓓ formal

IDENTIFY FIGURATIVE LANGUAGE

The underlined words in the sentences below are examples of figurative language. Choose the kind of figurative language used in each sentence.

1. My little sister is <u>as sly as a fox</u>.

    Ⓐ simile

    Ⓑ metaphor

    Ⓒ personification

2. When it comes to geography, Hiram <u>is a walking encyclopedia</u>.

    Ⓐ simile

    Ⓑ metaphor

    Ⓒ personification

3. How often in a day do you use the <u>information superhighway</u>?

    Ⓐ simile

    Ⓑ metaphor

    Ⓒ personification

4. The bus <u>waits patiently</u> for the elderly couple to board.

    Ⓐ simile

    Ⓑ metaphor

    Ⓒ personification

5. <u>As quick as a wink</u>, the thief had the jewels in his grasp and was out the window.

    Ⓐ simile

    Ⓑ metaphor

    Ⓒ personification

6. The parents were afraid that their child would use the <u>calculator as a crutch</u>.

    Ⓐ simile

    Ⓑ metaphor

    Ⓒ personification

7. My new job <u>fits me like a glove</u>.

    Ⓐ simile

    Ⓑ metaphor

    Ⓒ personification

8. The magnificent sunset <u>painted the sky</u> red, yellow, purple, and orange.

    Ⓐ simile

    Ⓑ metaphor

    Ⓒ personification

USE FIGURATIVE LANGUAGE (1)

In each sentence, underline the word or group of words that expresses an idea figuratively.

1. The exhausted soldiers marched like robots all the way back to camp.

2. After the rugged campaign, any smiling soldier would have stood out like a sore thumb.

3. As the late afternoon sun dipped below the horizon, the weary men and women reached camp.

4. The commander's eyes lit up like candles when he saw that all had returned safely.

5. Each soldier was tired and as hungry as a bear.

6. To each returning soldier, his or her small tent seemed as comfortable as an old shoe.

7. "I'll sleep like a log tonight," one said.

8. In the not-too-far distance, missiles exploded like thunderbolts.

9. But most of the brave and experienced soldiers remained as cool as cucumbers.

10. One nervous newcomer chattered like a monkey.

11. Another ran around like a chicken without a head, until an officer calmed him.

12. All night the wind howled through the camp.

13. The stars were diamonds sparkling in the vast sky.

14. One time, a flare went up overhead, and was as bright as the noonday sun.

15. The next morning, the soldiers' day began as the sun peeked out from behind the mountains.

16. The dense fog that had blanketed the valley lifted to reveal the large and active camp.

17. High up on its pole, the flag danced in the morning breeze.

18. "One thing is as clear as the nose on your face," one soldier remarked sadly. "The enemy is right where we left him yesterday and our work is cut out for us again today."

19. Most soldiers remained quiet, choosing to keep their feelings bottled up inside.

20. Soon, breakfast was over. Like the flick of a switch, the officers were calling out commands and the soldiers were at their posts, ready but not eager to face another long and grueling day.

Name ....

INTERPRET FIGURATIVE LANGUAGE

The sentences below contain figurative language. Each is a quote from an interview with George, who does not appear to see himself in the best light. Write, in your own words, what each sentence means.

1. From as far back as I can recall, sorrow has knocked at my door.

_____

2. For me, life has never been a bowl of cherries.

_____

3. Activities that some take to like fish to water are usually difficult for me.

_____

4. I am as meek as a lamb and as slow as molasses.

_____

5. Not only do I move like a snail, when I have to send a message, I use snail mail.

_____

_____

6. And even my computer is a dinosaur.

_____

_____

7. I don't even make a good couch potato.

_____

8. When I sing, I sing as flat as a pancake; when I dance, I have two left feet.

_____

9. The only thing that fits me like a glove is a glove.

_____

10. Even my bark is worse than my bite.

_____

Name ....

USE FIGURATIVE LANGUAGE (2)

Rewrite each sentence, enlivening it by adding a simile, a metaphor, or personification. Feel free to make additional changes to make your edits as smooth as silk.

1. With a splash, Redbird subway car #7835 took its final trip.

_____

_____

2. The 40-year-old subway car was dumped into the sea off the Delaware coast.

_____

_____

3. There, it will become an artificial reef where sea creatures can live.

_____

_____

4. The cause of its death was old age and the high cost of upkeep.

_____

_____

5. Dumping subway cars in the ocean was not the first solution for disposing of them.

_____

_____

6. One idea was to give them to needier subway systems around the world. But because the old cars contained asbestos within their walls, the plan was scrapped.

_____

_____

7. The Environmental Protection Agency approves of the plan, assuming that each car is cleaned thoroughly before it is dropped into the sea.

_____

_____

8. Other states like the idea of having the toxin-free cars dropped in the waters off their shores.

_____

_____

9. Owners of sport shops along those shores are very happy.

_____

_____

10. They'll soon be selling lots more fishing gear, because new reefs mean more fish.

_____

_____

Name ....

SENSORY IMAGES CHART

Sensory images are word pictures that appeal to our five senses.
First, complete the top chart by listing sensory details for Topic 1.
Use your imagination; think about what you might see, hear, smell, taste,
or touch by the water's edge. Then choose two other topics and fill in the
charts for each.

TOPIC 1: Description of a day at the seashore

SIGHTS	
SOUNDS	
SMELLS	
TASTES	
TOUCHES	

TOPIC 2: _____

SIGHTS	
SOUNDS	
SMELLS	
TASTES	
TOUCHES	

TOPIC 3: _____

SIGHTS	
SOUNDS	
SMELLS	
TASTES	
TOUCHES	

Name ....

CHOOSE THE SYNONYM

Read the sentence. Pick the word that is closest in meaning to the underlined word.

1. The reporter was asked to <u>revise</u> parts of her story.
- (A) erase
- (C) type
- (B) alter
- (D) discard

2. Writers often put their <u>faith</u> in their editor's good judgment.
- (A) manuscript
- (C) trust
- (B) religion
- (D) profits

3. Magazine writers mustn't be <u>tardy</u> when it comes to meeting their deadlines.
- (A) early
- (B) humorous
- (C) stingy
- (D) late

4. For a <u>novice</u>, her work is remarkably refined and professional.
- (A) nun
- (B) notary
- (C) beginner
- (D) veteran

5. Journalists must be <u>prudent</u> when reporting what certain sources tell them; providing misinformation can ruin reputations.
- (A) careful
- (B) careless
- (C) fearless
- (D) accurate

6. After doing what he thought was <u>sufficient</u> preparation, the journalist began the interview.
- (A) official
- (B) correct
- (C) lengthy
- (D) adequate

7. With the deadline rapidly approaching, the reporter called in her story with great <u>haste</u>.
- (A) fanfare
- (B) speed
- (C) excitement
- (D) delay

8. The official was suitably <u>penitent</u> after leaking classified information to an eager reporter.
- (A) unashamed
- (B) impoverished
- (C) humble
- (D) regretful

9. A good journalist will <u>persist</u> in her efforts to get at and report the truth.
- (A) resist
- (B) persevere
- (C) cease
- (D) cheat

10. The foreign news editor was <u>exultant</u> when the rebel leader agreed to an interview.
- (A) depressed
- (B) tired
- (C) elated
- (D) fired

Name ....

CHOOSE THE ANTONYM

Read the sentence. Pick the word that means the *opposite*, or very nearly the opposite, of the underlined word.

1. Composers should take it as a compliment when their work is compared to that of Mozart.
- (A) glorification
- (C) reduction
- (B) criticism
- (D) fulfillment

2. Stephen Foster may have been the first professional American songwriter.
- (A) acknowledged
- (C) learned
- (B) amateur
- (D) rookie

3. Lyricist William Gilbert and composer Arthur Sullivan created exceptional works together.
- (A) ordinary
- (B) abnormal
- (C) singular
- (D) operatic

4. The unique opening of *Oklahoma* affirmed the idea that the American musical could take a new and exciting direction.
- (A) asserted
- (B) solidified
- (C) declared
- (D) denied

5. At one time, New Orleans was the focus of the jazz world.
- (A) edge
- (B) axis
- (C) center
- (D) lens

6. The first Grammy Award for an album was given in 1958 to Henry Mancini for his theme for a TV program about a crafty detective.
- (A) clever
- (B) deceitful
- (C) hardworking
- (D) naive

7. The Rolling Stones grossed a staggering $121 million in their 1994 North American tour.
- (A) expected
- (B) bewildering
- (C) astonishing
- (D) steady

8. Enrico Caruso was one of the world's premier opera tenors in the early 20th century.
- (A) better
- (B) foremost
- (C) minor
- (D) beginning

9. Country singers and songwriters of today owe a hefty debt to Hank Williams, Sr.
- (A) slight
- (B) short
- (C) sizable
- (D) weighty

10. Johann Sebastian Bach left behind a prodigious body of music.
- (A) beautiful
- (B) unpleasant
- (C) bountiful
- (D) small

THESAURUS

Read each partial thesaurus entry. Each entry has one synonym (SYN) or antonym (ANT) that doesn't belong. Find this word and cross it out.

1. balmy [adj.] *comfortable with respect to weather*

SYN   mild, moderate, pleasant, refreshing

ANT   cool, harsh, inclement, tropical

2. confident [adj.] *certain, assured*

SYN   brave, convinced, fearless, negative

ANT   uncertain, unsure

3. discreet [adj.] *cautious, sensible*

SYN   careful, diplomatic, conservative, rash

ANT   careless, foolish, indiscreet, reckless

4. hostile [adj.] *mean, antagonistic*

SYN   belligerent, bitter, hateful, spiteful

ANT   agreeable, friendly, kind, malicious

5. interject [v.] *throw in, interrupt*

SYN   add, include, infuse, introduce

ANT   extract, intrude, remove, withdraw

6. mammoth [adj.] *huge*

SYN   colossal, enormous, giant, jumbo

ANT   little, miniature, monumental, small

7. mar [v.] *hurt, damage*

SYN   blemish, deface, deform, disfigure, maim

ANT   aid, heal, help, stain

8. oaf [n.] *person who is clumsy, stupid*

SYN   blunderer, brute, clod, dolt, fool, idiot

ANT   dunce, genius, intellectual, sage

9. prohibit [v.] *make impossible, stop*

SYN   ban, block, forbid, halt, impede, permit

ANT   allow, favor, grant, push

10. rigorous [adj.] *severe, exact*

SYN   accurate, brutal, harsh, meticulous

ANT   easy, easygoing, inflexible, lax, lenient

11. staid [adj.] *restrained, calm, sober*

SYN   composed, cool, dignified, sedate

ANT   adventurous, exuberant, frivolous, quiet

12. turmoil [n.] *chaos, commotion*

SYN   agitation, bedlam, confusion, order

ANT   calm, harmony, peace

USE ADJECTIVES AND ADVERBS

Write the letter of the correct form of the modifier to complete each sentence.

1. That is the _____ of the two mountain-bike courses.
   a. easy
   b. easier
   c. easiest
   d. more easier

2. It is the _____ of all the mountains in the range.
   a. high
   b. higher
   c. highest
   d. most highest

3. The skier's movements became _____ as she made her way down the slope.
   a. fluider
   b. more fluid
   c. more fluider
   d. fluidest

4. He practiced the _____ of any of the entrants in the halfpipe competition.
   a. little
   b. less
   c. least
   d. leastest

5. Her winning time in the giant slalom was the _____ time any racer had this year.
   a. fast
   b. faster
   c. fastest
   d. most fast

6. Thanks to the good weather, we hiked _____ this month than last month.
   a. often
   b. oftener
   c. more often
   d. most often

7. The trail was flat, so we rode much _____ than we had planned to.
   a. farther
   b. more far
   c. farthest
   d. more farthest

TOPIC SENTENCES AND SUPPORT

Read each topic sentence. Three of the four sentences that follow it support that topic sentence. Choose the sentence that *does not*.

1. Topic sentence: Gilroy, California, prides itself on being the "Garlic Capital of the World."

a. Every year there is a midsummer garlic harvest celebration in the town.

b. Many think that garlic is a particularly tasty addition to pizzas and pasta dishes.

c. Visitors to the annual Gilroy Garlic Festival can enjoy a garlic recipe contest and cook-off.

d. For information on the festival, contact www.gilroygarlicfestival.com.

2. Topic sentence: During the second week of September, Biscuits and Gravy Week is celebrated in San Antonio, Texas.

a. The annual Texas event honors this traditional marriage of foods.

b. Biscuits and gravy is a very popular dish in the southern and western parts of America.

c. The Homesteader Harvest Festival is held in South Dakota during this same week.

d. Throughout Biscuits and Gravy Week, hot biscuits are served with a wide variety of gravies.

3. Topic sentence: A folk singer, an American president, and a professional golfer are among those who were born on January 9.

a. Joan Baez was born on that date in 1941.

b. Sergio Garcia turned 22 on January 9, 2002.

c. On January 9, 1913, Richard Nixon was born.

d. Marcia Miller, co-author of this book, celebrates her birthday on January 9.

4. Topic sentence: The American Red Cross provides disaster relief at home and abroad.

a. International voluntary organizations provide invaluable help throughout the world.

b. This voluntary, not-for-profit organization was founded by Clara Barton on May 21, 1881.

c. Its 1.1 million volunteers collect and distribute blood.

d. Red Cross volunteers offer valuable health and safety information.

5. Topic sentence: Bowdler's Day is a time to recall the "contributions" of Thomas Bowdler, an English doctor born on July 11, 1754.

a. Bowdler was a self-righteous prude who devoted his time to "purifying" the works of Shakespeare by taking out all words and expressions he saw as indecent.

b. Bowdler also "cleansed" Gibbon's classic, *History of the Decline and Fall of the Roman Empire*, as well as some selections from the Bible.

c. A number of words in the English language come from people's names— think of all those figure-skating jumps, like the Salchow, Axel, and Lutz!

d. The term *bowdlerize*, meaning "to modify a work by removing all words or passages thought to be improper," has become part of the English language.

PARAGRAPHS AND TOPIC SENTENCES

Write a topic sentence for each group of related sentences.

1. The daffodils were beginning to appear alongside the purple, yellow, and white crocuses.
Most of the trees had begun to bud; a few were already leafed out.
The welcome crack of bats on balls could be heard throughout the park.

_____

_____

2. Many city streets were blocked off, snarling traffic for several blocks.
Hundreds of extra police officers were directing traffic and making the way safe.
People by the thousands lined the sidewalks and leaned out their windows.
The governor, the mayor, and many other civic leaders marched along with the floats.

_____

_____

3. It had rained all night and the morning's weather report forecasted continuing steady rain.
Signs posted throughout the National Park warned of the possibility of canyon flooding.
Downcast groups of hikers gathered at the trailheads, talking with rangers.
Some bolder hikers, who started down a trail, were now returning to the rim.
We decided to go have a leisurely breakfast and rethink our plan for the day's activity.

_____

_____

4. Some say that many years of drought made farming very difficult for the Anasazi, leading them to move away or to join other Native American groups.
Others point to evidence of invasions from the south and of violence in that region.
By about 700 years ago, all the Anasazi had left all their settlements in the Southwest.
Perhaps it was disease that did them in.

_____

_____

UNITY IN PARAGRAPHS

A paragraph has unity when all its sentences relate to its main idea.

First, read each paragraph to determine the main idea. Next, cross out the sentence that does not belong. Then explain why it does not belong.

1. Stoneware is a kind of ceramic. First made by the Chinese 3,500 years ago, stoneware got its name because it is fired at high temperatures to the consistency of stone. Eventually, potters throughout Asia learned and mastered the technology. In feudal Japan, for example, more than 80 regional kilns manufactured stoneware vessels. Wood ash from the firing melts to form a natural glaze, lighter in color than most glazes that potters apply.

_____

_____

2. Whether glazed or unglazed, stoneware makes excellent airtight and watertight containers. Over the centuries, the most practical use of stoneware was to make storage jars. Until recent times, stoneware storage jars were essential for many domestic and commercial needs. Jars held water, oil, wine, soy sauce, fish sauce, vinegar, pepper paste, salted fruits, and pickled vegetables. Potters used wooden anvils and paddles to create the thin-walled jars. The jars protected medicines, grains, and textiles from the insects and vermin that infested ships on long journeys. They also hid jewelry and coins.

_____

_____

3. Chinese stoneware jars had great value in some other cultures. For example, in Japan, they played a key role in the tea ceremony, _chanoyu_. The Japanese prized the jars' beautiful glazes and kept them as family heirlooms. In Iran, Syria, and other parts of western Asia, the potters used earthenware clay for making their storage jars. The Chinese jars also made their appearance in Vietnam and in Thailand, where they were used in religious ceremonies and valued for their colorful glazes.

_____

_____

USE TRANSITIONS

The ideas in a paragraph should be linked logically so that readers can easily see how one idea flows into the next. To make such connections and to carry readers' attention forward, writers use transitional words and phrases.

Choose the transitional word or phrase that best shows the relationship among the ideas in each sentence.

1. I usually don't eat chocolate, _____ that chocolate cake looked too good to pass up.
   a. like   **b.** but   **c.** therefore   **d.** since

2. I took a cooking class, and _____, I can now do more than boil water and make toast.
   a. however   **b.** similarly   **c.** most of all   **d.** as a result

3. The pepper mill is on the table _____ the saltshaker.
   a. due to   **b.** before   **c.** beside   **d.** namely

4. _____ I set the table, I sponged it down and wiped it dry.
   a. On the other hand   **b.** Thus   **c.** By contrast   **d.** Before

5. First, I put the water to boil, _____ I began making the sauce.
   a. then   **b.** in other words   **c.** here   **d.** in the very same way

6. I used several spices in the sauce, _____ sage, thyme, rosemary, and oregano.
   a. conversely   **b.** namely   **c.** on top of   **d.** unlike

7. I put in the pasta _____ the water in the pot came to a boil.
   a. therefore   **b.** as soon as   **c.** due to   **d.** like

8. The main course was very filling; _____ I had no room for dessert.
   a. because   **b.** finally   **c.** consequently   **d.** by contrast

9. My father eats only low-fat ice cream _____ he is on a diet.
   a. because   **b.** before   **c.** nevertheless   **d.** as a result

10. The bakery is _____ the corner from the drug store, next to the fish market.
   a. due to   **b.** unlike   **c.** below   **d.** around

COHERENT PARAGRAPH (1)

Read the paragraph. Think about how its ideas are related.
Then rewrite the paragraph by adding transitional words to connect
the ideas smoothly and logically.

In the game of golf, a player may use a maximum of fourteen clubs. There are three kinds of clubs. A "wood" has a head that is relatively broad from front to back and is usually made of wood, plastic, or a light metal. It is used for long shots. An "iron" has a head that is relatively narrow from front to back. It is usually made of steel. Irons are used for shorter shots. Woods and irons have one face for striking the ball. A "putter" is made of light metal. It is used for playing the ball once it is on or very near the putting green. Putters may have two striking faces. _____

_____

_____

_____

_____

_____

_____

_____

_____

Name ....

COHERENT PARAGRAPH (2)

Study the picture of the playing area for a curling match. Think about the visual information it provides and the relationships it shows. Then write a coherent paragraph that describes the playing area.

Curling Playing Area

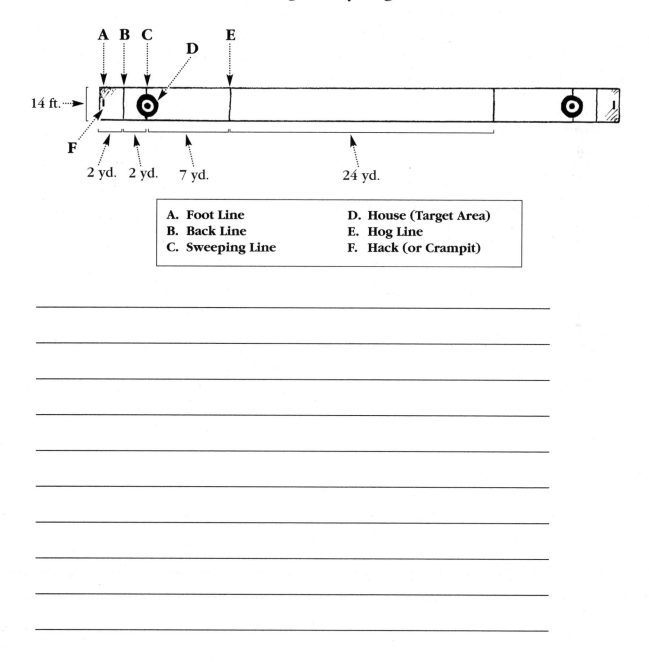

A. Foot Line	**D. House (Target Area)**
B. Back Line	**E. Hog Line**
C. Sweeping Line	**F. Hack (or Crampit)**

_____

_____

_____

_____

_____

_____

_____

_____

_____

_____

PART 3:

THE WRITING PROCESS

PREWRITING: NARROW A TOPIC (1)

If a topic you choose to write about is too broad, it will be hard for you to treat that subject thoroughly. Examine the sample of a topic made increasingly narrower:

BROAD TOPIC: Movies

NARROW TOPIC: Adventure movies

NARROWER TOPIC: Movies about adventures in the future

Complete the chart about narrowing given topics.

	BROAD	NARROW	NARROWER
1.	Team sports	Team sport played indoors	
2.	Desserts	Ice cream	
3.	Pets	Pet shops	
4.	Academy Awards	Academy Award for acting	
5.	African nations	Zimbabwe	
6.	American presidents	Theodore Roosevelt	
7.	Jobs		Stage manager
8.	Ocean life		Life along Australia's Great Barrier Reef
9.	Space travel	*Apollo* missions to the moon	
10.	Photography		Pioneering photographers
11.	The American West		Life along the Oregon Trail
12.		The giant panda	Worldwide efforts to save the giant panda

PREWRITING: NARROW A TOPIC (2)

You can use a topic web to help you narrow down a broad topic.

Complete the topic web below. Notice that the main topic appears within the center circle and subtopics go in circles that surround it. Narrower topics fill the outermost circles.

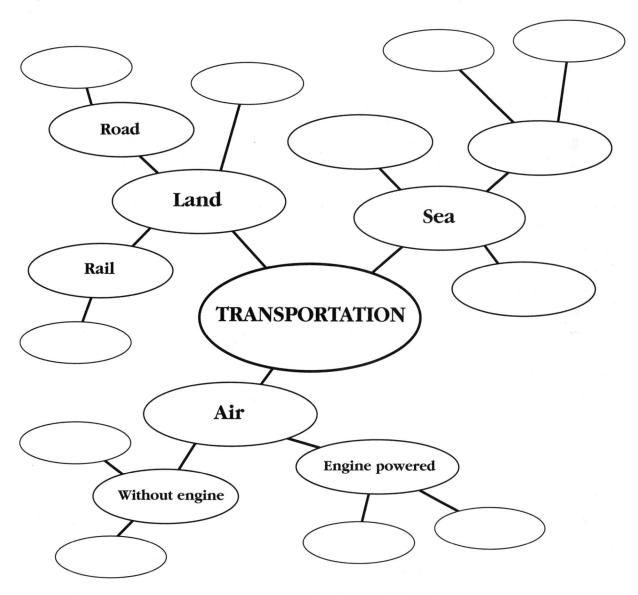

PREWRITING: NARROW A TOPIC (3)

You can use a topic web to help you narrow down a broad topic.

Complete the topic web below. Notice that the main topic appears within the center circle and subtopics go in circles that surround it. Narrower topics fill the outermost circles.

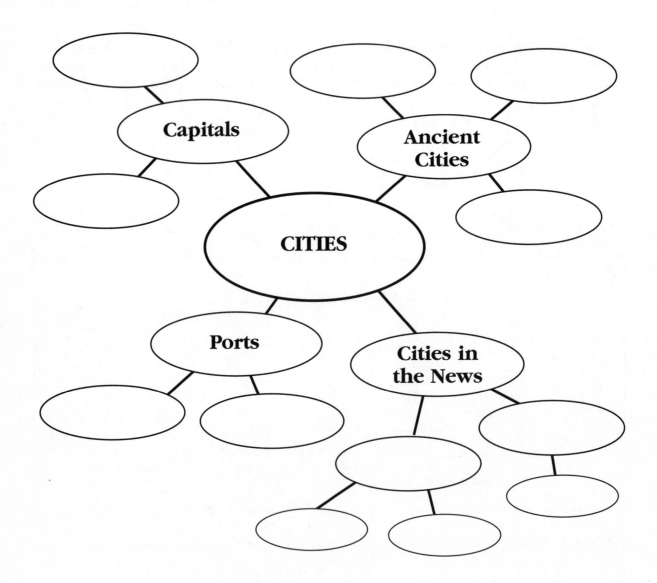

PREWRITING: USE A CHART TO GATHER DETAILS

You can use a word chart to gather specific details for a narrative. You can then use the words you record to vividly express your ideas.

Complete the chart below to describe a group white-water rafting trip.

Rafting Through the Grand Canyon on the Colorado River

Emotional Responses	Sensory Observations	Physical Reactions	Interpersonal Reactions
fear	tall, jagged red rock	wet as a sponge	trust

✳ CONNECT

Make another word chart for a different narrative writing topic. Use the chart to gather key ideas for different aspects of your topic. Or, focus on words for one aspect only, like *feelings*, and then divide that category into a few different headings, such as *joy*, *fear*, *anger*, and so on.

PREWRITING: USE A DIAGRAM TO GATHER DETAILS (1)

You can fill in a diagram to help gather details for a story or a poem.

Examine the diagram begun below for the main idea of *huge*. Notice that the key word appears in the center; related ideas are linked to it. Complete the diagram for *huge*.

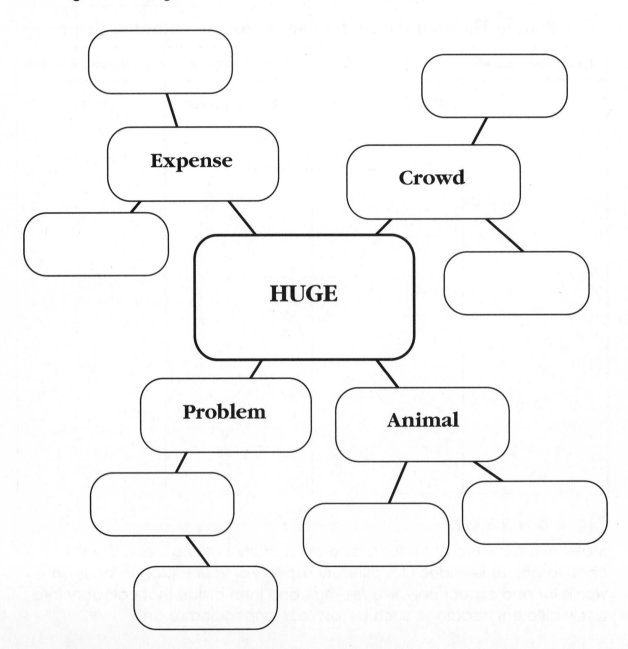

Name ....

PREWRITING: USE A DIAGRAM TO
GATHER DETAILS (2)

You can fill in a diagram to help gather details for a story or a poem. Think of an idea or feeling to express. Create and fill in a diagram for that idea or feeling.

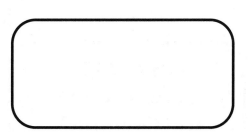

Name ....

PREWRITING: USE A DIAGRAM
TO GATHER DETAILS (3)

In the diagram below, the topic for a narrative is in the center.
Related ideas, feelings, and opinions connect to it. Study the diagram.
Then, on the next page, create a diagram of your own for a writing topic
of your choice.

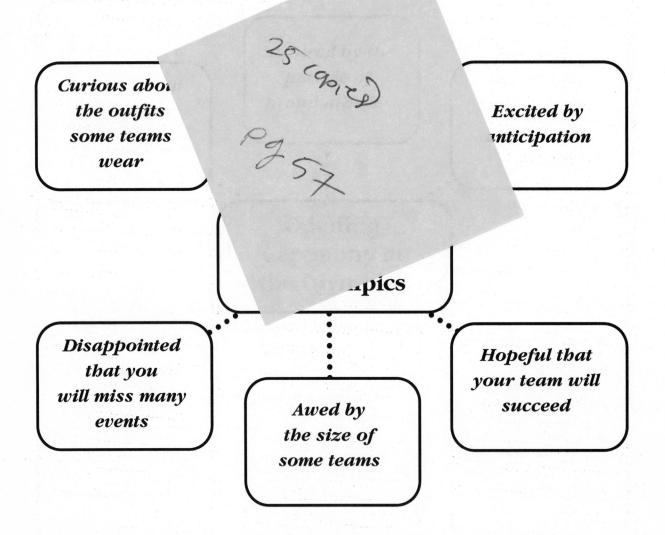

Name ....

PREWRITING: USE A DIAGRAM
TO GATHER DETAILS (3)

Create a diagram of your own for a writing topic of your choice.

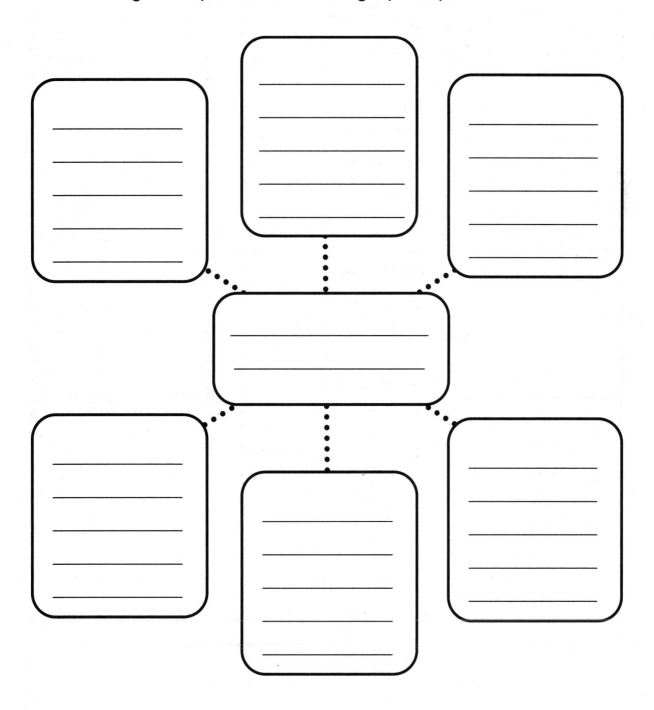

Name _____

PREWRITING: PARTS-OF-SPEECH WORD WEB

Use the word web to gather details for a descriptive passage you would write about a dramatic natural event, such as a volcanic eruption, an earthquake, a gale at sea, or a thunderstorm.

First, choose a topic. Then, list suitable nouns, verbs, adjectives, and adverbs where they belong.

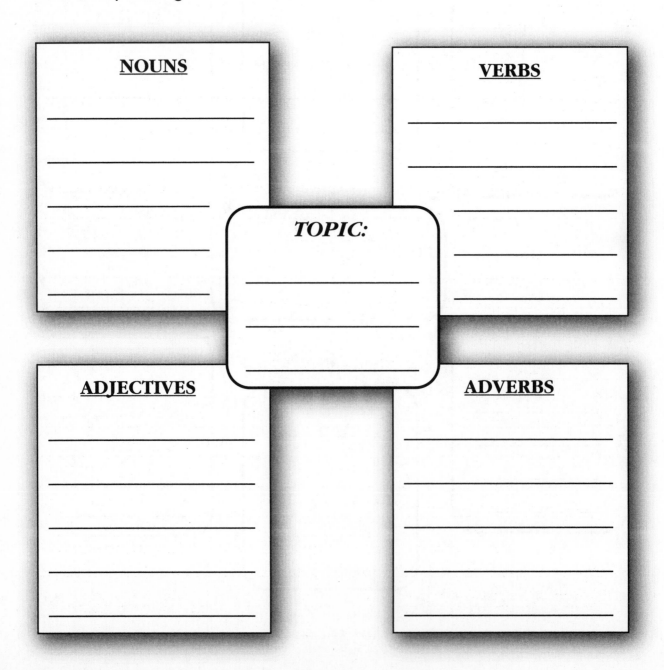

NOUNS

VERBS

TOPIC:

ADJECTIVES

ADVERBS

Name ....

PREWRITING: WHO, WHAT, WHERE, WHEN, WHY, AND HOW?

When you gather details for a report, biographical sketch, or other kinds of factual writing, it may help to list key questions. Your questions can guide your research and help you organize your findings.

First, choose a topic for a biographical sketch or a report. Then, write useful questions.

Topic: _____

WHO? _____

_____

_____

WHAT? _____

_____

_____

WHERE? _____

_____

_____

WHEN? _____

_____

_____

WHY? _____

_____

_____

HOW? _____

_____

_____

_____

PREWRITING: USE A CHART TO RESPOND TO LITERATURE

You can use a chart to gather and organize your response to literature by formulating questions. The questions you come up with can help you analyze the work thoroughly and thoughtfully. They can help you narrow your focus when you write.

Pick a book you have read or are reading now. Then write two or three questions you have about each of the categories listed.

BOOK TITLE: _____

AUTHOR: _____

PLOT: _____

_____

_____

_____

SETTING: _____

_____

CHARACTERS: _____

_____

_____

THEME: _____

_____

_____

WRITER'S CRAFT (i.e., style, language, literary devices): _____

_____

_____

LITERARY LINKS (other works like it): _____

_____

Name ....

PREWRITING: USE A CHART
TO ORGANIZE DETAILS (1)

A pros-and-cons chart helps you plan a persuasive essay. Weighing the reasons for and against your position can help you clarify—or even change—your views.

For each topic below, think about your opinion as well as possible contradicting views. Complete each chart. In the "Pros" column, list ideas that support your position. In the "Cons" column, list opposing views. Use additional paper if needed.

TOPIC 1: *Should the school year and day be lengthened? Yes ___ No ___*

Pros	Cons

TOPIC 2: *Should smoking tobacco be illegal? Yes ___ No ___*

Pros	Cons

TOPIC 3: *Should we cut spending on space exploration? Yes ___ No ___*

Pros	Cons

Name ....

PREWRITING: USE A CHART
TO ORGANIZE DETAILS (2)

You can use a T-chart to help you organize details for a problem/solution essay.

The charts below are started for you. Complete each one by adding relevant details.

1. Problem: Drinking Among Young People

Excuses Kids Give for Drinking	How to Solve the Problem
You have to do what your friends do to be cool.	Learn not to care what others think.

2. Problem: Too Many Injuries in High School Sports

Reasons for Injuries	How to Solve the Problem
Injuries are a part of sports.	Use better protective gear.

PREWRITING: SEPARATE FACT FROM OPINION

When you gather details for a report or any kind of composition, it is crucial to understand which details are facts and which are opinions.

Each statement below is about events preceding the American Revolution. Is the statement *fact* or *opinion*? Write F or O on the line next to each statement.

_____ **1.** The French and Indian War began in 1754 and lasted nine years.

_____ **2.** Colonists hated the 1765 Stamp Act more than they hated any other British action.

_____ **3.** Paul Revere's engraving of the Boston Massacre was the most masterful piece of propaganda of its time.

_____ **4.** In the early 1770s, some colonists boycotted English tea.

_____ **5.** No colonist was more resistant to British rule than Samuel Adams was.

_____ **6.** The First Continental Congress met in Philadelphia in 1774.

_____ **7.** Some colonists actively opposed independence from England.

_____ **8.** Nobody liked Thomas Paine, despite the importance of his pamphlet, *Common Sense*.

_____ **9.** Lord Dunmore, the governor of Virginia, offered to free any slaves and indentured servants who would leave their masters and fight for the British.

_____ **10.** Members of the Sons of Liberty always did the right thing at the right time.

_____ **11.** Paul Revere was the best of the several messengers entrusted with the key task of spreading news of British troop movements.

_____ **12.** The first shots of the war were fired at Lexington, Massachusetts, on April 19, 1775.

_____ **13.** The skirmish at Lexington was the most important day in American history.

_____ **14.** The battle on Breed's Hill was misnamed the Battle of Bunker Hill.

_____ **15.** George Washington's most important trait was his stamina.

✳ C O N N E C T

Look back at the statements you identified as opinions. On a separate sheet of paper carefully revise each one so that it becomes a statement of fact.

Name ....

PREWRITING: GATHER INFORMATION USING VARIOUS RESOURCES

Use a variety of resource materials when you gather information for a research paper.

Decide what kinds of sources are most appropriate for your topic. Choose the best answer.

1. You want to find a definition of *borough*.
Which resource would you use?

    a. an atlas   **b.** an almanac   **c.** a dictionary   **d.** an encyclopedia

2. You want to know which movie won an Oscar for best picture last year.
Which resource would be your best choice?

    a. an encyclopedia   **c.** a movie magazine Web site

    b. an almanac   **d.** an interview with someone who makes movies

3. You want to know the capital of Belgium. Which resource would help you?

    a. an almanac   **b.** an atlas   **c.** an encyclopedia   **d.** all of the above

4. You wish to know more about symptoms of the disease called *hepatitis*.
Which of the following resources would probably NOT be useful to you?

    a. a thesaurus   **c.** a physician-run hepatitis Web site

    b. a home medical guide   **d.** an interview with your doctor

5. You want to know about the life of a jellyfish. Which book is likely to help you the most?

    a. *Preserves and Marmalades*   **c.** *Life of Sea Mammals*

    b. *Encyclopedia of Ocean Creatures*   **d.** *Setting Up a Home Aquarium*

6. You are writing a report on the history of Kentucky's Mammoth Caves National Park. Which of the following resources would most likely be helpful?

    I. state of Kentucky Web site

    II. *Giant Mammals of the Past*

    III. National Park Service Web site

    IV. a geographical atlas

    a. all of the above   **b.** I and IV only   **c.** I, II, and III only   **d.** I and III only

DRAFTING: IDENTIFY THE AUDIENCE

Read each passage. Choose the audience for which it was written. Then explain your choice.

1. Auditions for the *Amici Cantorum* chamber choir will be scheduled at ten-minute intervals beginning at 6:00 P.M. on Thursday. Interested singers should bring a vocal résumé and prepare two pieces to perform—one in English and another in any other language. An accompanist will be available. Expect the music director to vocalize you to determine your range and quality of vocal production. Plan to sight-sing a short atonal *a cappella* work.

    a. experienced choral singers **b.** 7th-grade glee club members **c.** speech therapists

_____

2. Nicotine is the primary active ingredient in cigarettes, cigars, and chewing tobacco. It is highly addictive. When inhaled in small quantities, nicotine stimulates the central nervous system in much the same way that cocaine or amphetamines do. It causes the body to have higher levels of a chemical called dopamine. Dopamine carries signals to the brain and is linked with excitement. When smokers inhale nicotine, their heartbeats accelerate, their blood vessels constrict, and they feel relaxed. Nicotine also acts as an appetite suppressant. That explains why many people gain weight after they quit smoking.

    a. doctors   **b.** tobacco company executives   **c.** the general adult population

_____

3. There are two types of softball: slow pitch (SP) and fast pitch (FP), with a number of differences between the two. To begin with, the bases are 65 feet apart in SP and 60 feet apart in FP. In slow pitch, the mound is 46 feet from the plate, for both men and women. In fast pitch, that distance is 46 feet for men, but 40 feet for women. The outfield fence distances vary as well. For women, the fences are 200 feet in fast pitch and 250 feet in slow pitch. For men, those distances are 225–250 feet and 275–300 feet, respectively. Each fast-pitch or slow-pitch game lasts seven innings, but a game is official after five. A team consists of nine or ten players, any of whom can be substituted at any time. In contrast with hardball, all starting softball players who have been taken out of the game can reenter once. However, substitutes may not return once they have been removed.

    a. major league managers   **b.** people well acquainted with the game of baseball
    c. people unfamiliar with the game of baseball

_____

DRAFTING: KNOW YOUR TARGET AUDIENCE

Select a topic that is very familiar to you. Write TWO paragraphs about it: one for people who know as much about the topic as you do, and one for people who know little or nothing about it.

TOPIC: _____

1. Paragraph for Knowledgeable Audience

_____

_____

_____

_____

_____

_____

2. Paragraph for Uninformed Audience

_____

_____

_____

_____

_____

_____

DRAFTING: IDENTIFY AUDIENCE AND PURPOSE

Read the passage. Identify who its writer might be. Also describe its intended audience and purpose. Support your answer with specific details from the passage.

> Something has got to be done about the traffic lights along Westside Avenue! I know that it's a busy street and that there is an interest in keeping the traffic flowing. However, the city also must consider the needs of its pedestrians, particularly the many elderly who live in this neighborhood. They are suffering. For the elderly and the infirm, merely crossing this wide street before the light turns red is a difficult and potentially dangerous task. In the winter, when snow and ice make anyone's walk across that street a hazardous experience, our older citizens are totally helpless. What if they need to walk to their doctor or to pick up medicine at one of the drug stores on Broadway? Many simply stay home, too fearful of being unable to manage the daunting task before them. That's how bad the situation has become.
>
> This is an intolerable situation and you must act assertively now. Crossing a local street should not be a challenge for our taxpaying, law-abiding citizens. The traffic lights along Westside Avenue need to be adjusted for the benefit of all of us who live in the area and must cross that hazardous thoroughfare every day simply to run our errands and go about our daily lives. We voted for you last time because you promised that "quality of life" was the issue most dear to you. Now show us that you meant it. Show us that you care. People must cross that street to get to the voting booths, you know!

_____

_____

_____

_____

_____

_____

_____

_____

DRAFTING: HOW PURPOSE AFFECTS WRITING STYLE

Your purpose for writing should guide your choice of language and style. Examine the example below. It shows two sentences written on the same topic, but with a different purpose in mind.

TOPIC: A child in a Halloween costume

Purpose: To amuse	**Purpose:** To frighten
A kid dressed in a torn sheet skipped merrily up our front steps.	An absolutely terrifying phantom-like creature glided menacingly up our front steps.

Write two sentences on each given topic. Compose each sentence to serve a different purpose.

1. **TOPIC:** A TV star's performance

Purpose: To praise _____

_____

Purpose: To criticize _____

_____

2. **TOPIC:** A flight in a glider

Purpose: To excite _____

_____

Purpose: To warn against _____

_____

3. **TOPIC:** A friend's new hairstyle

Purpose: To compliment _____

_____

Purpose: To hide your dislike _____

_____

DRAFTING: CHOOSE THE ORGANIZING PLAN (1)

When you write, choose an organizing plan to present your topic clearly and effectively. The type of plan to use depends on your topic, your audience, and your purpose. Use transitions to support your organizing plan. Study the examples in the chart below.

Some Types of Organization	Some Common Transitions
Spatial Order	*below, next to, inside, in front of, beyond*
Chronological Order	*first, next, then, before, after, recently*
Order of Importance	*primarily, most important, in addition*
Cause and Effect	*therefore, thus, due to, because, if, then*

Read each passage and answer the questions that follow.

Before you do anything else, preheat the oven to 425°F. Then gather all the listed ingredients. Next, fill the duck cavity with a mixture of apple, onion, and celery pieces. Then place the duck breast-side up on the rack in a shallow roasting pan and sprinkle it with salt. After you've baked the duck for 15 minutes, reduce the oven temperature to 325°F. From then on, baste every 10 minutes. Bake for a total of 1 1/2 hours, until the duck is tender.

1. Which organizing plan has the writer used? _____

2. How do you know? _____

_____

3. Why does this plan suit this topic? _____

_____

The contest area for the indoor Olympic sport of judo is a large square mat called a *shiaijo*. Around the mat is a 1-meter-wide red danger area surrounded by a safety area of green matting. The contestants face each other, standing four meters apart. All their movements take place within the contest area. A referee, who generally remains within that area, governs the contest. Two judges assist the referee from opposite corners of the safety area. Coaches and fans remain outside the entire contest area.

4. Which organizing plan has the writer used? _____

5. How do you know? _____

_____

6. Why does this plan suit this topic? _____

_____

DRAFTING: CHOOSE THE ORGANIZING PLAN (2)

Use organizing plans—chronological order, order of importance, spatial order, and cause and effect—to help readers understand how your ideas are related.

Read the passage below. Answer the questions that follow.

A slight tilt in the earth's axis will change the angle at which the sun's rays strike the planet. Even a small wobble can cause temperatures to rise or drop. If temperatures drop, then winds lift evaporated moisture from oceans and later deposit it as snow in high altitudes. This causes glaciers to enlarge. These huge bodies of ice lock up so much water that sea levels fall. Where sea floors are shallow to begin with, continental shelves can be exposed. And that is exactly what happened to the Bering Sea thousands of years ago—it drained like a sink and became a grassy plain.

Onto this plain came animals, followed by people who hunted them. Both were fleeing the spreading ice in Siberia. But then temperatures rose and ice began to melt, causing water to fill the plain once more. Its occupants fled for higher ground and safety. The western part of the plain flooded first; thus the people and the animals were forced to go east—to Alaska and Canada. So, due to what we now know about past climate changes, we understand that the first inhabitants of North America were not explorers looking for a new world. Rather, they were refugees, escaping a natural disaster and just trying to survive.

1. Which organizing plan has the writer of the passage used?

_____

_____

2. How do you know?

_____

_____

3. Why does this plan suit this topic?

_____

_____

DRAFTING: CHOOSE THE ORGANIZING PLAN (3)

Use organizing plans—chronological order, order of importance, spatial order, and cause and effect—to help readers understand how your ideas are related.

Read the passage below. Answer the questions that follow.

Let me not mince words: The play was simply awful. To begin with, the acoustics in the theater were poor. We had a hard time hearing the actors from our uncomfortable seats way in the back, practically in the theater's lobby. From whatever we could see and hear, it became clear that few of the actors could act. Many of them couldn't even recall their lines. Furthermore, some were badly miscast. In addition, the set was unimaginative and the costumes were boring. However, a more significant problem was the play itself. This was far from the playwright's best effort. Her plot was tired, her dialogue was dull, and few characters were fully developed. How disappointing. But the worst thing of all was the astronomical ticket price!

1. Which organizing plan has the writer of the passage used?

_____

2. How do you know?

_____

_____

_____

3. Why does this plan suit this topic?

_____

_____

_____

_____

REVISING: EDIT FOR PARALLELISM

When using conjunctions in writing, connect only sentence elements that are alike. This repetition of a grammatical form is called *parallelism*. For example, linking nouns with nouns and keeping verb forms alike provides a pleasant rhythm.

Each sentence contains faulty parallelism. Rewrite it to fix the problem.

1. One summer we vacationed along the shores of Florida, Georgia, the Carolinas, and along the Virginia shore.

_____

_____

2. While snorkeling I saw angelfish, barracuda, and parrot fish were swimming around.

_____

_____

3. Most of the beaches we encountered were sandy, but there were also some rocky beaches. _____

_____

4. At one beach we watched a sea bird locate its prey, circling above it, and swiftly diving down to grab it.

_____

_____

5. We spent an entire afternoon looking for a beach with reefs for good snorkeling and that had snorkeling equipment to rent.

_____

_____

6. The colors in the water off one Florida beach included dark blue, light blue, patches where the water was pale green, and turquoise.

_____

_____

REVISING: VARY SENTENCE LENGTH IN PARAGRAPHS

Writing is more interesting with variations in the structure and length of sentences. To vary the structures, mix simple, compound, and complex sentences. To vary the lengths, add more examples, descriptive details, and observations.

Rewrite the following paragraphs to make them more interesting. You may combine, revise, or reorder the sentences.

Pluto is the only planet that was discovered by an American. Clyde Tombaugh detected it in 1930. He did so at the Lowell Observatory in Flagstaff, Arizona. It was a very exciting discovery. In the following year Walt Disney renamed his lovable cartoon dog after it. But is Pluto a planet? Astronomers disagree.

There are several reasons why there is confusion. First of all, Pluto is hard to see. Pluto is very, very small, too. It is much smaller than our moon. It stands by itself in other ways. Four of the planets are rocky bodies. Four are gas giants. But Pluto is an ice ball. It is very far from the sun. It is the only planet not yet visited by a probe from Earth. Recently, astronomers found comets, asteroids, and other bodies orbiting the sun that are larger than Pluto. They are closer to the sun, too. Is Pluto one of these rather than a planet? An answer to this question depends on how astronomers agree to define what planets are. The jury is still out on this decision. One thing seems clear. Pluto is the misfit in the family of planets.

_____

_____

_____

_____

_____

_____

_____

_____

_____

REVISING: ENLIVEN DULL SENTENCES

Read the two sample sentences.

Boring sentence: The hungry boy ate a meat sandwich.

Better sentence: The ravenous boy wolfed down a ham on rye in two enormous bites.

The dull sentences that follow need your help. Add precise nouns, vivid verbs, and lively adjectives and adverbs. If possible, use similes, metaphors, and personification.

1. The opening day of each new baseball season is a big deal.

_____

_____

2. It was a nice day at the large, crowded ballpark.

_____

_____

3. The mayor threw the fake first pitch to the home team's big catcher.

_____

_____

4. Fans agree that they like the sound of the bat hitting the ball.

_____

_____

5. When the favorite player got an important hit there was clapping and loud cheering in the place.

_____

_____

6. All sighed when another player struck out with two outs and three runners on base.

_____

_____

7. The fielder made a very good catch while running toward a wall.

_____

_____

8. The game lasted a long time and the score was close the whole way.

_____

_____

Name ....

REVISING: FIX A TERRIBLE COMPOSITION

The passage that follows is simply awful! It is full of grammatical errors as well as punctuation, capitalization, and spelling mistakes. In addition, there are errors in sentence structure and style. And if that is not bad enough, some of the sentences are so dull, they may put you right to sleep! Read the passage carefully. Then, on a separate sheet of paper, rewrite it to correct its many problems.

Easter island is a unique place. It be a ruggedly beautiful land of volcanic rock in the Pacific Ocean, just 14 miles long and 7 miles wide. Located about 2000 miles from Chile in South America and about 1000 miles from Pitcairn Island in the South Pacific. Easter Island is 1 of the most isolated places on Earth. It got the name by whom we know it when Dutch explorer Jacob Roggeveen, came upon it on Easter Day in 1,722. But earlier settlers called the island Te Pito O Te Henua, which meaning Navel of the World. Today, the people of Easter Island call theirselves, their land, and their language Rapa Nui. The island is mostly known by far for the enormous stone statues, called *moai*, that dot it's Coastline.

Easter Islands history has long been the subject of speculation. Now they are under Chilean influence and has a population of about 2000. But where did its original inhabitants come from? Why did the islanders carve the massive statues in the first place. Once they carved these giants, how did they transports them to where they stand all over the island? And what remains of that advanced and puzzling culture. Which included rock carvings wood carvings and the only written language in Oceania? Furthermore, why did the population, which once exceeded 10,000, recline at one point to about 100?

The great norwegian adventurer Thor Heyerdahl saw a similarity between the stone art and architecture on Easter Island and that of Indian ruins in Peru and Bolivia. Based on that observation, he proposed that the original Easter Islanders had sailed there from South America. However, more recent archaeological evidence indicate otherwise. The evidence shows that Polynesians discovered and began settling the island in about 440 ad. It shows that the people of the small island dropped when it began to exceed the capabilitys of its ecosystem: Resources became scarce. And the islanders faced disaster. In also, evidence shows that the once thriving Island fell into decline. Then to Civil War and chaos.

Today, Easter Island remains one of the coolest places on Earth, it is an open-air museum in a pretty landscape of archaeological sights, lava formations, and volcanic craters? It is a markable exhibit of a lost culture. Visit the Easter Island home page for lynx to more information about this nice place.

PART 4:

WRITING ACTIVITIES

- **Exposition** is writing that informs, explains, or gives information.

- **Narration** is writing that tells a story.

- **Persuasion** is writing that tries to convince others.

- **Expression** is writing that conveys thoughts and feelings from one's experience.

- **Report Writing** presents research information on a given topic. It is a form of exposition.

- **Response to Literature** is writing that gives thoughtful reactions to literature.

- **Practical Writing** is real-life writing.

Name ....

WRITING: EXPOSITION (1)

Write one of the following:

- **A description of the traits of a good child-care worker or baby-sitter**

- **A description of the responsibilities of a director of a play, movie, or music video**

- **A description of the qualities of a true friend**

Use the steps of the writing process as you work:

1. Gather and organize your ideas and details.

2. Choose your audience and purpose.

3. Draft your composition. Use more paper as needed.

4. Edit for content and style.

5. Proofread for grammar, spelling, punctuation, and capitalization errors.

_____

_____

_____

_____

_____

_____

_____

_____

WRITING: EXPOSITION (2)

Write one of the following:

- **An explanation of how to plan a surprise party**
- **Instructions for cooking something just the way you like it**
- **Instructions for how to guide a beginner to use in-line skates**

Use the steps of the writing process as you work:

1. Gather and organize your ideas and details.

2. Choose your audience and purpose.

3. Draft your composition. Use more paper as needed.

4. Edit for content and style.

5. Proofread for grammar, spelling, punctuation, and capitalization errors.

_____

_____

_____

_____

_____

_____

_____

_____

_____

_____

Name ....

WRITING: EXPOSITION (3)

Write one of the following:

- **A comparison of your daily life with that of a celebrity you admire**

- **A summary of the plot of a movie, television program, novel, or short story**

- **An evaluation of an athlete's performance**

Use the steps of the writing process as you work:

1. Gather and organize your ideas and details.

2. Choose your audience and purpose.

3. Draft your composition. Use more paper as needed.

4. Edit for content and style.

5. Proofread for grammar, spelling, punctuation, and capitalization errors.

_____

_____

_____

_____

_____

_____

_____

_____

_____

Name ....

WRITING: EXPOSITION (4)

Write one of the following:

- **An evaluation of a product you use and like (or dislike)**

- **A solution to the problem of noise pollution in big cities**

- **Advice to someone who has trouble being on time**

Use the steps of the writing process as you work:

1. Gather and organize your ideas and details.

2. Choose your audience and purpose.

3. Draft your composition. Use more paper as needed.

4. Edit for content and style.

5. Proofread for grammar, spelling, punctuation, and capitalization errors.

_____

_____

_____

_____

_____

_____

_____

_____

_____

_____

_____

WRITING: NARRATION (1)

Write one of the following:

- **A description of a hard decision you have made**

- **A description of someone who is special to you**

- **A description of a humorous family experience**

Use the steps of the writing process as you work:

1. Gather and organize your ideas and details.

2. Choose your audience and purpose.

3. Draft your composition. Use more paper as needed.

4. Edit for content and style.

5. Proofread for grammar, spelling, punctuation, and capitalization errors.

_____

_____

_____

_____

_____

_____

_____

_____

_____

_____

_____

_____

_____

WRITING: NARRATION (2)

Write one of the following:

- **An anecdote that shows your individuality or creativity**
- **A description of a big change you or someone you know has undergone**
- **A recollection of a frightening or comical personal experience**

Use the steps of the writing process as you work:

1. Gather and organize your ideas and details.

2. Choose your audience and purpose.

3. Draft your composition. Use more paper as needed.

4. Edit for content and style.

5. Proofread for grammar, spelling, punctuation, and capitalization errors.

_____

_____

_____

_____

_____

_____

_____

_____

_____

_____

_____

_____

_____

WRITING: PERSUASION (1)

Write one of the following:

- **A letter to the editor of the local newspaper on the need for better public transportation**

- **An essay recommending the installation of more bicycle racks in shopping areas**

- **Pointers for a teacher who is new to your school**

Use the steps of the writing process as you work:

1. Gather and organize your ideas and details.

2. Choose your audience and purpose.

3. Draft your composition. Use more paper as needed.

4. Edit for content and style.

5. Proofread for grammar, spelling, punctuation, and capitalization errors.

_____

_____

_____

_____

_____

_____

_____

_____

_____

_____

Name ....

WRITING: PERSUASION (2)

Write one of the following:

- **A speech you would give if you were running for president of the student body**

- **A press release advertising a music group you like**

- **A public service announcement asking people to use water sparingly during a shortage**

Use the steps of the writing process as you work:

1. Gather and organize your ideas and details.

2. Choose your audience and purpose.

3. Draft your composition. Use more paper as needed.

4. Edit for content and style.

5. Proofread for grammar, spelling, punctuation, and capitalization errors.

_____

_____

_____

_____

_____

_____

_____

_____

_____

_____

WRITING: EXPRESSION (1)

Write one of the following:

- **An anecdote about when something unexpected happened to you**

- **A journal entry about something that angered you**

- **An e-mail or letter to a friend you haven't seen or spoken to in six months**

Use the steps of the writing process as you work:

1. Gather and organize your ideas and details.

2. Choose your audience and purpose.

3. Draft your composition. Use more paper as needed.

4. Edit for content and style.

5. Proofread for grammar, spelling, punctuation, and capitalization errors.

_____

_____

_____

_____

_____

_____

_____

_____

_____

_____

Name ....

WRITING: EXPRESSION (2)

Write one of the following:

- **A letter to a historical figure**

- **A personal memoir about an event from your early childhood**

- **An anecdote about something remarkable a pet (or baby brother or sister) did**

Use the steps of the writing process as you work:

1. Gather and organize your ideas and details.

2. Choose your audience and purpose.

3. Draft your composition. Use more paper as needed.

4. Edit for content and style.

5. Proofread for grammar, spelling, punctuation, and capitalization errors.

_____

_____

_____

_____

_____

_____

_____

_____

_____

_____

WRITING: EXPRESSION (3)

Write one of the following:

- **A letter to a chef describing a food you ate**

- **A letter to a movie executive telling why a certain actor is the one to play you in a movie**

- **A postcard written during a pleasure trip on the space shuttle**

Use the steps of the writing process as you work:

1. Gather and organize your ideas and details.

2. Choose your audience and purpose.

3. Draft your composition. Use more paper as needed.

4. Edit for content and style.

5. Proofread for grammar, spelling, punctuation, and capitalization errors.

_____

_____

_____

_____

_____

_____

_____

_____

_____

_____

Name _____

WRITING: REPORT WRITING

Choose one of these topics on which to write a report:

- **A famous composer, musician, or artist from the past**
- **The Lewis and Clark expedition of 1804**
- **The history of tennis**
- **A country in southeast Asia**
- **Modern exploration of the ocean floor**
- **A guide to Rocky Mountain recreation opportunities**
- **Piloting a hot-air balloon**

Don't write the report yet. Explain how you would proceed to research and write it. Focus on answering these questions:

1. What led you to choose this topic?

2. How and where would you gather your data?

3. What sources would you use?

4. How would you record and organize your data?

5. What style and content issues would you focus on when you draft your report?

6. How would you document and cite your reference sources?

_____

_____

_____

_____

_____

_____

_____

Name ....

WRITING: RESPONSE TO LITERATURE

Write one of the following:

- **Advice to a character in a book or short story**
- **A letter to an author or illustrator of a book you enjoyed (or disliked)**
- **A review of a book, story, play, or poem for the school newspaper**

Use the steps of the writing process as you work:

1. Gather and organize your ideas and details.

2. Choose your audience and purpose.

3. Draft your composition. Use more paper as needed.

4. Edit for content and style.

5. Proofread for grammar, spelling, punctuation, and capitalization errors.

_____

_____

_____

_____

_____

_____

_____

_____

_____

_____

WRITING: PRACTICAL WRITING

Write one of the following:

- **A message to record on an answering machine at a small business**

- **A letter to a local store offering your after-school services making bicycle deliveries**

- **A bulletin-board message giving the rules for using a public swimming pool**

Use the steps of the writing process as you work:

1. Gather and organize your ideas and details.

2. Choose your audience and purpose.

3. Draft your composition. Use more paper as needed.

4. Edit for content and style.

5. Proofread for grammar, spelling, punctuation, and capitalization errors.

_____

_____

_____

_____

_____

_____

_____

_____

_____

_____

WRITER'S SELF-EVALUATION CHECKLIST

Refer to this checklist to help you improve your writing.

- ❏ Is your purpose clear?

- ❏ Have you written for your intended audience?

- ❏ Does your introduction grab readers?

- ❏ Did you get across your main ideas?

- ❏ Have you stuck to your topic?

- ❏ Do you offer enough details, descriptions, facts, or other information?

- ❏ Have you cut out unnecessary details?

- ❏ Is your point of view consistent throughout?

- ❏ Have you used complete sentences?

- ❏ Is your piece presented in sensible or logical order?

- ❏ Have you used transitions to help your piece flow smoothly?

- ❏ Have you varied sentence style and length?

- ❏ Does your conclusion work?

- ❏ Do your characters make sense? Do they speak and act as you wish them to?

- ❏ Have you described the setting?

- ❏ Have you included sensory details?

- ❏ Can you substitute vivid verbs, exciting adjectives, and other precise words?

- ❏ Have you indented new paragraphs?

- ❏ Have you proofread for grammar, spelling, capitalization, and punctuation?

TEACHER NOTES AND SELECTED ANSWERS

Part 1: Grammar and Mechanics

Sentences and Sentence Problems (p. 8)

1. d 2. a 3. c 4. a 5. a 6. c 7. d 8. a 9. b
10. a

Write Complete Sentences (p. 9)

Many answers are possible. All sentences should have subjects and verbs. Some need independent clauses added.

Write Sensible Sentences (p. 10)

1. C 2. B 3. D 4. B 5. C Guide students to look for cause-effect relationships. Emphasize to students that they should not change the meanings of the sentences when they combine them.

Fix Run-On Sentences (p. 11)

Answers will vary. Students should use coordinating conjunctions (i.e., *and*, *but*, *or*, *for*, *nor*) to join independent clauses. They can use semicolons to link two closely related independent clauses.

Common Nouns and Proper Nouns (p. 12)

Answers to 1–16 will vary, but all proper nouns should begin with capital letters, song titles should appear within quotations, and movie titles should be in italics. Sample answers: 17. country 18. artist 19. poet 20. constellation 21. baseball team 22. continent 23. basketball player 24. car company 25. singer 26. state 27. river 28. month 29. novel 30. play 31. baseball stadium 32. inventor

Identify Kinds of Nouns (p. 13)

1. b 2. a 3. c 4. d 5. a 6. a 7. a 8. c 9. a
10. b 11. a 12. c 13. d 14. a 15. b 16. b 17. c
18. b 19. a 20. d

Nouns: General, Specific, and More Specific (p. 14)

Sample answers: 2. robin 3. jeans 4. relative 5. food 6. computer, laptop 7. movie, horror movie 8. drink, orange soda 9. book, mystery 10. comedy, *Dumb and Dumber* 11. TV show, news program 12. fictional character, cartoon character

Use Abstract Nouns (p. 15)

1. b 2. c 3. a 4. d 5. b 6. c 7. a 8. d 9. b
10. c

Use Pronouns (p. 16)

You may wish to review types of pronouns: personal, demonstrative, relative, and interrogative. 1. b 2. c
3. d 4. b 5. a 6. c 7. b 8. c 9. b 10. b

Pronouns and Antecedents (p. 17)

Point out that pronouns may precede their antecedents. 1. b 2. c 3. a 4. d 5. c 6. b 7. c
8. d

Use Pronouns Correctly (p. 18)

1. Incorrect 2. Incorrect 3. Incorrect 4. Correct
5. Incorrect 6. Correct 7. Incorrect 8. Correct
9. Incorrect 10. Correct

Identify the Simple Predicate (p. 19)

1. B 2. B 3. A 4. D 5. B 6. D 7. C 8. A 9. A
10. C 11. C 12. A

Use the Right Verb Form (p. 20)

Guide students to watch for irregular verb forms. Discuss that using the wrong verb form can spoil the effect of what a writer means to get across.

1. c 2. b 3. d 4. d 5. c 6. b 7. d

Use Linking Verbs (p. 21)

A linking verb connects a subject with a word that describes or identifies it. Other linking verbs: become, appear, feel, grow, look, seem, stay, sound, taste, smell, turn, remain. 1. c 2. c 3. b 4. d 5. d
6. c 7. d

Forms of Adjectives and Adverbs (p. 22)

You may wish to review the distinction between the comparative and superlative forms of modifiers and between adjectives and adverbs themselves. Discuss cases of the use of *more* and *most* with modifiers. 2. highest 3. speedier 4. least 5. painful
6. sharper 7. most slowly 8. cautious 9. better, best 10. bad 11. friendlier, friendliest 12. more flexible, most flexible 13. shallow, most shallow
14. easier, easiest 15. powerful, more powerful

Use Prepositional Phrases (p. 23)

Answers will vary. Discuss with students how prepositional phrases make space and time relationships more clear.

Find the Spelling Errors (p. 24)

1. B 2. C 3. A 4. D 5. E 6. D 7. E 8. B 9. D
10. C 11. A 12. E

Find Capitalization Errors (p. 25)

1. C 2. D 3. E 4. C 5. B 6. D 7. A 8. D 9. E
10. D 11. E 12. B

Correct Punctuation Errors (p. 26)

Sample answers: 1. Donald, who generally eats only burgers and pizza, won a prize of a dinner for himself and three friends at a gourmet restaurant. 2. "Which of my pals should I invite?" Donald wondered. 3. After some thought, he settled on Juan, Julie, and Pat. 4. The only one of the four with a more sophisticated palate than Donald was Pat, whose diet also included pasta, tacos, and even some vegetables. 5. For dinner at the city's top-rated restaurant, each friend dressed up and looked fantastic! 6. "Wow!" Juan exclaimed, when he saw

the limo pull up to take them to their meal.
7. Julie's first problem at the restaurant was not
knowing which fork to use for the first course:
stuffed mushrooms and baby sweet pickles.
8. Actually, no one in the group was ever sure which
utensil to use with each of the five courses.
9. Finally, the dessert arrived: a chocolate mountain
floating in a lake of raspberry sauce. 10. On the
next day, while the four friends waited in line at a
fast-food joint, they agreed that the previous night's
main course could've used some ketchup.

Complete the Sentence: Homophones (p. 27)
Review what homophones are. 1. They're 2. reign
3. site 4. capital 5. all ready 6. assistants 7. cruise
8. course 9. missed 10. sighed 11. sign
12. patience 13. role 14. You're 15. review
16. soar 17. We've 18. chord 19. rout 20. meet

Write a Sentence: Homophones (p. 28)
Sentences will vary; make sure they make sense.

What's Wrong With the Sentence? (p. 29)
1. C 2. A 3. D 4. B 5. C 6. B 7. D 8. B

Part 2: Writing Styles

Identify the Tone (p. 32)
1. B 2. C 3. D 4. A 5. C 6. D 7. C 8. B

Identify Figurative Language (p. 33)
1. A 2. B 3. B 4. C 5. A 6. A 7. A 8. C

Use Figurative Language (1) (p. 34)
1. like robots 2. like a sore thumb 3. dipped
4. like candles 5. as hungry as a bear 6. as
comfortable as an old shoe 7. like a log 8. like
thunderbolts 9. as cool as cucumbers 10. like a
monkey 11. like a chicken without a head
12. howled 13. diamonds sparkling 14. as bright as
the noonday sun 15. peeked out 16. blanketed
17. danced 18. as clear as the nose on your face
19. bottled up 20. like the flick of a switch

Interpret Figurative Language (p. 35)
Students' sentences will vary; check that each
expresses the gist of the given sentence.

Use Figurative Language (2) (p. 36)
Students' sentences will vary. You may wish to do
one or two sentences together with the whole class.

Sensory Images Chart (p. 37)
Students' sensory details will vary. You may wish to
brainstorm sensory details for Topic 1 together with
the class.

Choose the Synonym (p. 38)
Point out to students that a synonym given may be
for only one meaning of a word with many meanings. 1. B 2. C 3. D 4. C 5. A 6. D 7. B 8. D
9. B 10. C

Choose the Antonym (p. 39)
Point out to students that an antonym given may be
for only one meaning of a word with many meanings.
1. B 2. B 3. A 4. D 5. A 6. D 7. A 8. C
9. A 10. D

Thesaurus (p. 40)
As needed, help students read a thesaurus entry.
1. tropical 2. negative 3. rash 4. malicious
5. intrude 6. monumental 7. stain 8. dunce
9. permit 10. inflexible 11. quiet 12. order

Use Adjectives and Adverbs (p. 41)
1. b 2. c 3. b 4. c 5. c 6. c 7. a

Topic Sentences and Support (p. 42)
1. b 2. c 3. d 4. a 5. c

Paragraphs and Topic Sentences (p. 43)
Discuss the idea that topic sentences can appear
anywhere in a paragraph; brainstorm or find together
examples of paragraphs in which the topic sentences
are not the opening sentences. Sample answers:
1. Spring had arrived. 2. The city readied itself for
the parade. 3. The trails in the park were unsafe for
hiking. 4. We don't know for sure why the Anasazi
disappeared from the Southwest.

Unity in Paragraphs (p. 44)
1. Wood ash from the firing melts to form a natural
glaze, lighter in color than most glazes that potters
apply. 2. Potters used wooden anvils and paddles to
create the thin-walled jars. 3. In Iran, Syria, and
other parts of western Asia, the potters used
earthenware clay for making their storage jars.

Use Transitions (p. 45)
Review how transitional words express relationships
among ideas. Focus on the most common
arrangements among related ideas in paragraphs,
such as chronological order, spatial order, order of
importance, and so on. Review the transitional words
commonly used to show those relationships. 1. b
2. d 3. c 4. d 5. a 6. b 7. b 8. c 9. a 10. d

Coherent Paragraph (1 & 2) (pp. 46-47)
Students' paragraphs will vary. Look for transitional
words and phrases that show comparison or
contrast in (1); for (2), look for those that show
spatial relationships.

Part 3: The Writing Process

Prewriting: Narrow a Topic (1) (p. 50)
Answers will vary. You may wish to have students
work in small groups to extend the activity: one
student suggests a topic, another narrows it, and a
third narrows it further.

Prewriting Activities (pp. 51-62)

Have groups of students share and discuss their charts and diagrams. For p. 59, emphasize the wide range of potentially helpful questions students might ask; provide or elicit examples, such as "Who influenced the person and helped her to become the person she was?" or "What good qualities does your subject have?" For p. 60, you may help get students started with sample plot questions, such as "Who did the action?" or character questions like "Who does the character remind you of?" For pp. 59-62, you may wish to extend the activities by having students write compositions based on their prewriting work.

Prewriting: Separate Fact From Opinion (p. 63)

1. F   2. O   3. O   4. F   5. O   6. F   7. F   8. O   9. F   10. O   11. O   12. F   13. O   14. F   15. O.   For the Connect activity, it may be helpful to demonstrate a revision. For example, for sentence 5, suggest "Several historians have written that no colonist...."

Prewriting: Gather Information Using Various Resources (p. 64)

1. c   2. b   3. d   4. a   5. b   6. d   Ask students to defend their choices.

Drafting: Identify the Audience (p. 65)

1. a; Only experienced choral singers would understand the specific musical language.   2. c; The information and language is too simplistic for doctors; the information most likely is known by tobacco company executives.   3. b; The reader is expected to know the meaning of some baseball-specific words.

Drafting: Know Your Target Audience (p. 66)

Have students share their passages and explain why they are appropriate for their chosen audience. Invite classmates to listen and make suggestions.

Drafting: Identify Audience and Purpose (p. 67)

Sample answer: The writer resides in the Westside Avenue neighborhood and is writing to a government representative, perhaps the local congressperson. The purpose of the passage is to inform that representative of a troublesome situation that urgently needs to be remedied.

Drafting: How Purpose Affects Writing Style (p. 68)

Have students share their sentences. Invite classmates to comment on the sentences' effectiveness in meeting the writer's intended purpose.

Drafting: Choose the Organizing Plan (1) (p. 69)

1. chronological order   2. time order, indicated by words such as *before*, *next*, *then*, and *after*   3. Transitional words indicating time order are appropriate because when cooking, you need to follow steps in a particular order, often having to wait for one part of the process to end before you begin the next step.   4. spatial order   5. words and

phrases such as *large square*, *area*, *surrounded by*, *within*, *opposite corners*, *outside*   6. Using transitional words indicating spatial relationships helps the reader to visualize the setting of a judo contest.

Drafting: Choose the Organizing Plan (2) (p. 70)

1. cause and effect   2. transitional words such as *if...then*, *therefore*, and *thus*   3. Transitional words indicating cause and effect are appropriate because the passage is about how climatic changes impacted the settling of North America.

Drafting: Choose the Organizing Plan (3) (p. 71)

1. order of importance   2. words and phrases such as *to begin with*, *furthermore*, *in addition*, and *but the worst thing of all*   3. The reviewer criticizes aspects of the play in reverse order of importance, in order to more effectively make his or her argument.

Revising: Edit for Parallelism (p. 72)

You may wish to review examples of parallel structures. Sample answers: 1. One summer we vacationed along the shores of Florida, Georgia, Virginia, and the Carolinas.   2. While snorkeling I saw angelfish, barracuda, and parrot fish.   3. Most of the beaches we encountered were sandy, but some were rocky.   4. At one beach we watched a sea bird locate its prey, circle above it, and swiftly dive down to grab it.   5. We spent an entire afternoon looking for a beach with both reefs for good snorkeling and snorkeling equipment to rent.   6. The colors in the water off one Florida beach included dark blue, light blue, pale green, and turquoise.

Revising: Vary Sentence Length in Paragraphs (p. 73)

Revisions will vary. Look for students' use of transitional words and punctuation changes to affect the changes in sentence lengths. Encourage more able students to also vary sentence beginnings as well as structures. Guide all students to read each full paragraph before editing it.

Revising: Enliven Dull Sentences (p. 74)

Revisions will vary.

Revising: Fix a Terrible Composition (p. 75)

Sample answer:

Easter Island is a unique place. It is a ruggedly beautiful land of volcanic rock in the Pacific Ocean, just 14 miles long and 7 miles wide. Located about 2,000 miles from Chile in South America and about 1,000 miles from Pitcairn Island in the South Pacific, Easter Island is one of the most isolated places on Earth. It got the name by which we know it when Dutch explorer Jacob Roggeveen came upon it on Easter Day in 1722. But earlier settlers called the island "Te Pito O Te Henua," which means "Navel of the World." Today, the people of Easter Island call themselves, their land, and their language Rapa Nui.

The island is best known, by far, for the enormous stone statues, called *moai*, that dot its coastline.

Easter Island's history has long been the subject of speculation. Now it is under Chilean influence and has a population of about 2,000. But where did its original inhabitants come from? Why did the islanders carve the massive statues in the first place? Once they carved these giants, how did they transport them to where they stand all over the island? And what remains of that advanced and puzzling culture, which included rock carvings, wood carvings, and the only written language in Oceania? Furthermore, why did the population, which once exceeded 10,000, decline at one point to about 100? The great Norwegian adventurer Thor Heyerdahl saw a similarity between the stone art and architecture on Easter Island and that of ancient Indian ruins in Peru and Bolivia. Based on that observation, he proposed that the original Easter Islanders had sailed there from South America. However, more recent archaeological evidence indicates otherwise. The evidence shows that Polynesians discovered and began settling the island in about 440 A.D. It shows that the population of the small island dropped when it began to exceed the capabilities of its ecosystem: Resources became scarce and the islanders faced ecological disaster. In addition, the evidence shows that the once thriving social order fell into decline and then to civil war and chaos.

Today, Easter Island remains one of the most unique places on Earth. It is an open-air museum in a mesmerizing landscape of archaeological sites, lava formations, and volcanic craters. It is a remarkable exhibit of a lost culture. Visit the Easter Island home page for links to more information about this fascinating place.

Part 4: Writing Activities

Writing: Exposition (pp. 78–81)

Students' passages will vary. Look for a stated purpose or thesis in an introduction and/or conclusion, knowledge of the topic, and a logical and effective organizational plan.

Writing: Narration (pp. 82–83)

Students' narrations will vary. As appropriate, look for an established setting and situation, a conflict and resolution, a point of view, and developed characters. In rich compositions, the narration will be unified and engaging, and the student will have used a variety of narrative devices such as dialogue, tension, suspense, vivid verbs and modifiers, precise nouns, figurative language, and expressions.

Writing: Persuasion (pp. 84–85)

Students' compositions will vary. Look for a structure in which details, reasons, examples, and anecdotes are arranged persuasively and appropriately for the intended audience. Look for arguments supported by detailed evidence (with cited sources as needed) and the exclusion of irrelevant information or argument. Strong persuasive essays develop readers' interest, have a controlling idea that conveys a judgment, and anticipate and address possible reader concerns and counter arguments.

Writing: Expression (pp. 86–88)

Students' passages will vary. Anecdotes may be informally written, can be short and humorous, and may provide the writer's personal observations about life. Journal entries are often written for the writer's eyes only, may be informal and therefore contain sentence fragments or even single words. They often express feelings, and should be dated. Personal letters, e-mails, or postcards are informal, dated, and should contain salutations, bodies, and closings. Postcards should be brief and should not include "private" information. All of these three kinds of expression should present factual news as well as feelings and opinions. Personal memoirs are remembrances of events from the past. They should contain emotional responses as well as details, and are generally written in the first person.

Writing: Report Writing (p. 89)

Students' responses will vary. Check that they have fully addressed each question. Check that students' chosen sources make sense for the topic they have selected, that their organizational plan logically suits the topic, and that their stylistic issues and content goals are appropriate.

Writing: Response to Literature (p. 90)

Students' compositions will vary. In the letter to the author, students should feel free to make suggestions and to offer constructive criticism. The letter may be written in the style of a personal letter. In their responses to a book, story, play, or poem, students may give their overall reactions or they may focus only on elements of interest to them.

Writing: Practical Writing (p. 91)

Students' messages and letters will vary. Check that the answering-machine message provides essential and useful information and that it is brief, clear, and businesslike. Check that the job-request letter uses precise language and that it has the form and concise style of a business letter. Check that the bulletin board message provides key information in a logical order.